ARK ON
THE MOVE

ARK ON THE MOVE

Gerald Durrell

Coward-McCann, Inc.
New York

Published by
Coward-McCann, Inc.
200 Madison Avenue
New York, NY 10016

Conceived, edited and produced by
Nicholson Books
10 Price Street
Toronto, Ontario
Canada M4W 1Z4

**Library of Congress Cataloging in
Publication Data**
Durrell, Gerald Malcolm, 1925-
  Ark on the move.
1. Zoology — Madagascar.   2. Zoology —
Mauritius.   3. Endangered species —
Madagascar.   4. Endangered species —
Mauritius.   5. Scientific expeditions —
Madagascar.   6. Scientific expeditions —
Mauritius.   I. Title.
QL337.M2D87
1983   591.969'1   82-8261
ISBN 0-698-11211-3

Designed by Maher & Murtagh

Printed in Spain by Printer
industria gráfica s.a.
Barcelona   D.L.B. 12823-1983

By the same author

THE OVERLOADED ARK
THREE SINGLES TO ADVENTURE
THE BAFUT BEAGLES
THE DRUNKEN FOREST
MY FAMILY AND OTHER ANIMALS
ENCOUNTERS WITH ANIMALS
A ZOO IN MY LUGGAGE
THE WHISPERING LAND
TWO IN THE BUSH
BIRDS, BEASTS AND RELATIVES
FILLETS OF PLAICE
CATCH ME A COLOBUS
BEASTS IN MY BELFRY
THE STATIONARY ARK
THE AMATEUR NATURALIST
ROSY IS MY RELATIVE
THE MOCKERY BIRD
THE NEW NOAH
ISLAND ZOO
LOOK AT ZOOS
MY FAVOURITE ANIMAL STORIES
THE DONKEY RUSTLERS

This is for
Monsieur Le Professeur Roland Albignac
otherwise known to us as
Professor "Pas De Problème"
without whose help we could
have achieved little.

Contents

slowly dying ecologically. Yet business thrives at the fabulous Zoma market. Contact is made with the charming tenrec and several graceful lemurs.

The expedition moves out to the special sanctuary of Berenty for a unique meeting with the extraordinary ring-tailed lemur and its cousins. Kites, sifakas, snakes and cockroaches abound. At another reserve, Ankarafantsika, progress is made more hazardous by the spiky tree trunks. A dart gun is used to capture a few lemurs, and an arduous night mission turns up a nocturnal avahi.

A visit is made to the great thorny forest around Hazofotsy, a weird landscape populated by the very odd alluaudia and baobab trees, the miniature mouse lemur, the spider tortoise, and the screeching lepilemur. The island of Nosy Komba greets the expedition with enthusiasm. A great feast is prepared for the visitors, and exotic dances begun. A special tribute is paid to the island's sacred lemur colony.

Back in mainland Madagascar, the expedition sets out for Perinet to search for the noble indri. There is much to see along the way, from zebu, butterflies, frogs, chameleons, to carniverous plants. A tired crew beds down in a decrepit but utterly charming old hotel. The search begins, and after an exhausting sweep of the forest, the expedition is literally ambushed by a troop of indri. An unexpected and fulfilling end to the voyage.

Foreword

Even the most cautious of travellers would, I think, be thrilled at the idea of visiting a remote tropical island. There seems to be something about tropical islands that stirs the blood of even the most unadventurous souls. So you can imagine how excited Lee, my wife, and I were when we got the chance to visit not just one but four tropical islands in the Indian Ocean, and one of them uninhabited at that. Let me explain how this piece of luck came about.

I have been associated with islands, one way or another, for most of my life and became island mad — a confirmed islomaniac — at a very early age by being brought up on the wonderful Greek island of Corfu. It was here that I could first indulge my passion for natural history, and I scoured the island, both on my donkey and in my boat, to secure specimens for my home museum and live creatures to keep and study. Everything from eagle owls to sea-horses, from snakes to scorpions, was grist to my mill. Naturally this early training made me want to see more of the world and its plant and animal life, so I became an animal collector for zoos and travelled far and wide and met and brought back to Europe an enormous variety of fascinating creatures. But after a few years I became dissatisfied for two reasons. Firstly, I disliked having to part with my animals at the end of a trip, and secondly, I was not sure that the zoos I dealt with were properly oriented.

As I travelled all over the world I could see how animal life was becoming more and more endangered by the encroachment of man. In the case of many species, their numbers had been so drastically reduced in the wild state, either by hunting pressures or by habitat destruction, that I knew it would be impossible for them to recover unaided. What these harried creatures needed were sanctuaries where they could live and breed in safety and recover their numbers. This sort of sanctuary should, I thought, be provided

Gerald and Lee Durrell with some of the Ring-tail lemurs bred in captivity at Jersey.

Les Augrès Manor, World
Headquarters of the Jersey
Wildlife Preservation Trust.

by zoological gardens, but in most cases the zoos in
question were not far-sighted enough to realize that
they were probably the last hope for the survival of
many magnificent animals. So I decided to found a zoo
of my own, on the island of Jersey, one of the Channel
Islands. It was to be a zoo with a difference, one that
concentrated on the breeding of endangered species
with the hope that, when their numbers had built up
sufficiently and they were out of danger, some of the
captive-bred specimens could be released back into
their native habitat to bolster wild populations, or to
reintroduce the species into areas where it had become
extinct. So I founded the Jersey Wildlife Preservation
Trust, a scientific organisation whose headquarters is
the Jersey Zoological Park, to carry out this important
and urgent rescue work.

A few years ago we made a TV series called *The
Stationary Ark* on our work and our success in breeding
everything from gorillas to rare and endangered birds
and reptiles. This series was a great hit and so we were
asked to make another one. In this new series, called
Ark on the Move, we were to show not only our breeding successes but our rescue operations in the wild.
Also, we wanted to show our new scheme for working
with governments all over the world to save their
animals and to bring people from these countries to
Jersey for training in the complex and difficult art of
captive breeding. All these creatures should really be

bred in their country of origin, but often this is impossible because of a lack of expertise in these countries. Thus, in fact, Jersey has become the first mini-university of captive breeding as an aid to conservation. So we were to visit Mauritius, Rodrigues and Round Island in the Mascarenes, where we were already working with the Government, and then to visit the fabulous island of Madagascar to see what help we could give there.

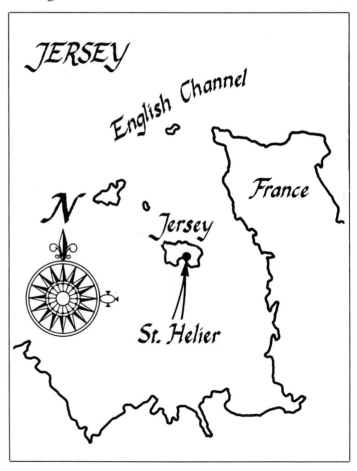

The island of Jersey.

Madagascar and the Mascarene islands.

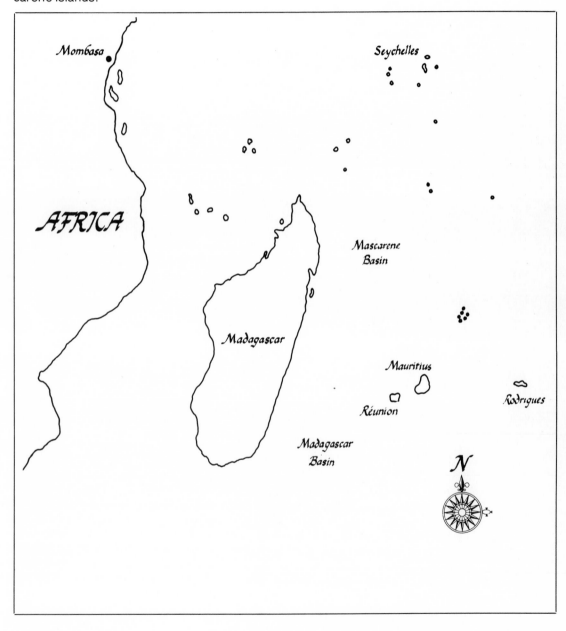

Landing
on the
Dodo's Grave

The trip was to be great fun in many ways, but particularly because John Hartley, my assistant, and I knew the Mascarene Islands well and so I was greatly looking forward to showing them to Lee. For her part she had spent two years in the Malagasy forests studying animal communication for her PhD thesis, and was therefore looking forward to showing us the fabulous Malagasy fauna.

Our connection with Mauritius really began when we decided to adopt the dodo as the Trust's symbol. When Mauritius was discovered by Europeans it had a unique bird fauna found nowhere else, and probably the most curious of these was the great, flightless, harmless dodo, a large bumbling bird the size of a goose, some say related to the pigeon. The dodo, being flightless, nested on the ground, and, having no enemies, was quite tame and fearless. As soon as man arrived, it had enemies in plenty, ranging from man himself to the various domestic creatures and pets he rapidly introduced. The dodo could not cope with this influx of enemies; within a hundred years of its discovery it had vanished, leaving only a few bones. So the sad phrase 'as dead as a dodo' entered the language. The dodo's fate seemed to sum up the way mankind was treating many different species all over the world, and this is why we chose it as our symbol.

We spent an exciting couple of months preparing for our trip. Maps and reference works had to be consulted, equipment like binoculars, recording machines and cameras checked, and tropical clothing dragged out of moth-balls and examined with a critical eye. At last the day came and we set off from Jersey on the first leg of our journey, a freezing day with driving rain, the sort of day that made you yearn for the tropics, and we couldn't wait to get there.

It is a curious sensation when your huge aircraft lands at Plaisance Airport in Mauritius, for you know you are landing on the dodo's graveyard. Beneath the

The Common Dodo discovered in the 1500s and exterminated within a 100 years, has now been adopted as the symbol of the Jersey Trust.

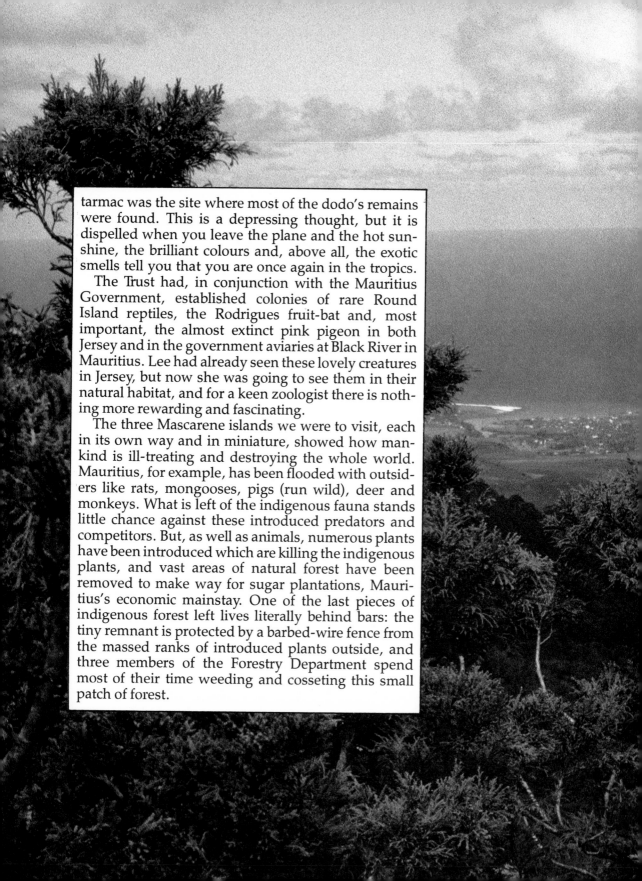

tarmac was the site where most of the dodo's remains were found. This is a depressing thought, but it is dispelled when you leave the plane and the hot sunshine, the brilliant colours and, above all, the exotic smells tell you that you are once again in the tropics.

The Trust had, in conjunction with the Mauritius Government, established colonies of rare Round Island reptiles, the Rodrigues fruit-bat and, most important, the almost extinct pink pigeon in both Jersey and in the government aviaries at Black River in Mauritius. Lee had already seen these lovely creatures in Jersey, but now she was going to see them in their natural habitat, and for a keen zoologist there is nothing more rewarding and fascinating.

The three Mascarene islands we were to visit, each in its own way and in miniature, showed how mankind is ill-treating and destroying the whole world. Mauritius, for example, has been flooded with outsiders like rats, mongooses, pigs (run wild), deer and monkeys. What is left of the indigenous fauna stands little chance against these introduced predators and competitors. But, as well as animals, numerous plants have been introduced which are killing the indigenous plants, and vast areas of natural forest have been removed to make way for sugar plantations, Mauritius's economic mainstay. One of the last pieces of indigenous forest left lives literally behind bars: the tiny remnant is protected by a barbed-wire fence from the massed ranks of introduced plants outside, and three members of the Forestry Department spend most of their time weeding and cosseting this small patch of forest.

The ease with which a plant (or an animal) can be introduced into a country and wreak havoc is epitomised in Mauritius by the tale of the strangler liana. We went one day to visit the huge and beautiful botanical gardens at Pamplemousses near the capital, Port Louis. Here our friend, Wahab Owadally, Chief Conservator of Forests, showed us this remarkable plant. The liana has habits similar to those of the European ivy, except that it literally strangles its host. Just one of these deadly plants was introduced by chance to Mauritius, but that was quite enough to do the damage. As Wahab explained, the seeds of the liana are shaped rather like miniature helicopters and so are widely dispersed by the wind. When the seed lands and germinates, the young plant searches out a tree and then, wrapping itself round like a python, it proceeds to climb up its host and slowly strangle it. As the tree dies and rots, it leaves the strangler triumphant, like a great mass of coiled springs.

The giant lily pads at the botanical gardens.

Our main task in Mauritius in the past has been to try and save the beautiful pink pigeon from extinction. It is curiously ironical that the only breeding grounds of this beautiful bird were discovered in a remote valley, situated—above everything else—in a small grove of cryptomeria, a fir-like tree which was imported to Mauritius as a source of timber. This small group had been planted in such remote and difficult terrain that the trees could not be got out of the valley, and so they grew and flourished and were taken over by the pink pigeon as its nesting site.

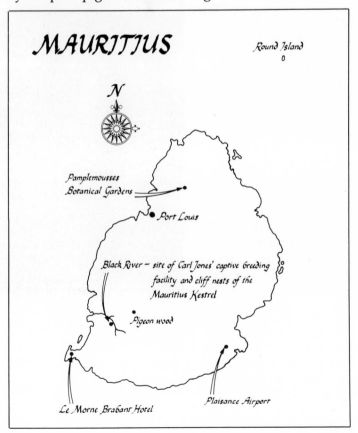

Getting into the pigeon wood was a tiring and laborious process. In the early morning when you start out it is generally raining and the mountains are enveloped in cloud. This turns the ground into a quagmire. For part of the way the narrow path leads through waist-high undergrowth and you are soon soaked to the skin. Then the path dips, steep and slippery as a roller coaster, down into the valley, running through dense groves of Chinese guava and traveller's palms that look like huge green Victorian fans stuck, half open, in the ground. Finally, sopping wet, covered with mud and bitten to death by a million mosquitoes, you reach the gloomy cryptomeria grove.

In the higher branches of the trees the Forestry Department had constructed platforms, with rough ladders leading up to them. From these high vantage points one was able to keep a watch on practically the whole world population of pink pigeon. All around you could hear the throaty, purring cries of the birds, a lovely slumberous sound. Gradually, as the sun gets higher, the clouds and mist break up and then, in the brilliant light, the trees gleam with raindrops like a million diamonds and the various shades of green dazzle the eye. The pink pigeons are extraordinarily tame creatures and will come and perch within a few feet of you, cooing to each other, bobbing their heads and touching their beaks together in a ritual 'kiss', their lovely throats and breasts glowing pale cyclamen pink in the sun, their wings and tails as russet-red autumn leaves.

A bird's eye view, deep in the forest, of the spiky sanctuary of the pink pigeon.

The beautiful pink pigeon in its natural habitat.

Although the wild population of the pink pigeon has dwindled to about ten birds, some seventy-five have been bred in captivity, such as this lovely specimen.

In 1976, when John and I arrived in Mauritius, the wild population of pink pigeon was estimated at thirty-five. There were also three birds in captivity, but no signs of breeding. The Mauritian Government decided it was only sensible to try to get some more. This presented us with some difficulties, for it was not the breeding season, the easiest time to catch them. However, we tried to turn their extraordinary tameness to good account. With the aid of the Government's special mobile force, we entered the grove of cryptomeria at dusk and marked down where the birds were going to roost. Then when it was dark we dazzled them with a portable searchlight. This, together with their natural lack of fear, allowed us to shin up into the cryptomeria to try to catch them with a strange net device that looked rather like gigantic sugar tongs. This sounds simple but was in fact laborious, difficult and dangerous, for the cryptomeria branches were brittle and you were operating sometimes fifty feet off the ground. However, by this means we did manage to catch one bird which was added to the three at Black River. During the next year's breeding season, John returned to Mauritius to try for more specimens and with the aid of a *bàl-chatri* he caught eight birds. A *bàl-chatri* looks like an old-fashioned bell-shaped meat safe, covered with fine nylon nooses. This is placed over the nest and the bird flying in to incubate alights on it and gets its legs caught by the nooses. Three of these birds were left at Black River and five came to Jersey. Since then, the wild population has dwindled to about ten birds, but our safety measures have paid off and there are now seventy-five birds in captivity, of which twenty-four are in Jersey.

The purpose of this trip was to work out which birds from Jersey should be sent back to Mauritius and which from Mauritius should be sent for breeding to Jersey. When you are dealing with such a tiny gene pool for a species of animal it is essential that you try to cross your bloodlines as much as possible in an attempt to prevent in-breeding and all its attendant risks. Carl Jones, a dedicated and most amusing young ornithologist, is in charge of the Black River project and, together with Yousoof Mungroo (a Mauritian trained in Jersey) he has worked out a huge genealogical chart on which we could trace the lineage of every captive pink pigeon: when it was hatched, who its parents and grandparents were and who it is married to. We brooded over this complex chart so that, as Carl said, we looked as though we were arranging marriages for some minor European royalty. But this was much more interesting and worthwhile.

Carl Jones, the dedicated ornithologist, in charge of the Black River conservation project.

When the final choices were made, we caught up the pigeons and packed them carefully in stout cardboard boxes for the journey. Naturally, with such a rare and important cargo they could not travel alone. John was to accompany them to Jersey and, when they were safely settled in, rejoin us for the next stage of the trip. Any tourist who thinks explaining a couple of bottles of Scotch and a few cartons of cigarettes to a gimlet-eyed customs officer is difficult should try explaining a few cardboard boxes full of pink pigeons. The task is complex to say the least. We finally got John and the birds on the plane, leaving a series of customs officials with grave doubts as to our sanity. It was wonderful to watch the plane take off and know that another chapter in the saga of trying to save the pink pigeon had ended successfully. It made us realise once again how important the work we were doing in Jersey was, both in breeding the different endangered species and in training people to carry on the work in places like Mauritius.

Another species that Carl is struggling to save in the Black River aviaries is what must surely be the rarest bird of prey in the world, the Mauritian kestrel, whose numbers in the wild state have been cut down to fifteen pairs. The reasons for the decline of this bird are complex. One of the factors is that some of the kestrels like to nest in holes in trees, while others prefer the high cliff ledges in the great central gorges of Mauritius. The ones that nest in the trees, of course, have their eggs and nestlings preyed upon by the introduced Macaque monkeys, cunning and skilful predators. The ones that nest on the remote cliff ledges are comparatively safe. But there is another and more important reason for the little hawk's decline, and that is that, strangely enough, it is being driven to extinction by introduced plants. This may sound ridiculous, but it is nevertheless true. The original Mauritian forest is rapidly declining, pushed out and strangled by a myriad of introduced plants and trees. In the native Mauritian forest lives the main food source of the kestrel, the Phelsuma lizards. These brilliantly beautiful lizards, dragon-green, decorated in scarlet and black spots, abound in places where original forest still clings on. They scuttle to and fro up the tree trunks and lie sunning themselves in the branches, looking like some fantastic Christmas decorations modelled from emeralds and rubies. These little reptiles are not only ravishing to look at but must taste good as well, for the kestrel hunts them almost to the exclusion of everything else. But as the forest diminishes so does the lizard population, and a pair of kestrels needs an awful lot of the five-inch long reptiles to feed a brood of two or three babies as well as themselves. This is a good example of how, indirectly, mankind all over the world is altering and destroying nature. With the careless introduction of foreign trees and plants the native forest perishes (as the dodo perished when faced with dogs, cats, pigs and monkeys) and as the forest goes, the Phelsuma vanishes, affecting as it does so the last link in the chain, the kestrel. But there is some hope, for other species of kestrels have been bred successfully in captivity. So with luck Carl will be able to establish a viable breeding group of this, the rarest bird

Hanging precariously to the edge of a remote cliff, members of the expedition watch for the Mauritian kestrel.

The Mauritian kestrel, one of the rarest birds of prey in the world, shown here both in the wild and in captivity. Only fifteen pairs of these exotic birds remain in their natural state.

of prey. Once again, it seems as though through captive breeding the Mauritian kestrel, like the pink pigeon, may be saved and not follow the dodo into oblivion.

While we waited for John to return from Jersey I took the chance of showing Lee the reef. To any zoologist a coral reef is one of the most fantastic sights in the world, for not only are the coral formations themselves so incredible, like the most bizarre, colourful and complex baroque architecture, but the creatures that inhabit these beautiful underwater landscapes are equally unbelievable. Every day we snorkeled for two or three hours on the reef and every day we saw at least four or five species of fish we had not seen previously. We were bedazzled by the shapes and colours of the fish, the corals and all the other sea life that inhabited the coral groves in millions.

But at last our holiday came to an end, for John returned and we had to make plans for visiting our second island, the uninhabited Round Island, home of rare sea birds, strange palm trees and unique reptiles.

The Dying
Island

One of the chief problems for reptiles is that this vast group of fascinating and useful creatures has had a very bad press since the Garden of Eden reportage hit the headlines. Most people shudder when you mention reptiles and are under the erroneous impression that all snakes and other cold-blooded creatures are slimy, poisonous and malign. In fact they are not slimy, but dry and cool to the touch like a snakeskin handbag. They only turn on you if you tread on them or threaten them, and you would do the same. Finally, of the myriad reptile forms in the world only a tiny proportion are poisonous. They are all of them, even the poisonous ones, of great benefit to mankind in eating insect pests and rodents. It has been calculated that the number of snakes killed in India per annum would, if left to themselves, devour so many rats and mice that the Indian people would benefit by the saving of millions of tons of grain that these rodents eat.

We are very proud of our magnificent reptile breeding facility in Jersey, particularly as we obtained it in a curious way. Raising money for the conservation of animals is always difficult, but it's comparatively simple if you've got something cute and cuddly like the giant panda. Because of their undeserved reputation, to raise money for snakes and lizards and tortoises is very difficult indeed. Which is why, for a long time, we had to house our reptiles in a converted garage. Then one year we held a conference, the first world conference on the breeding of endangered species in captivity. During the course of the meeting a Canadian member of the Trust approached me.

'Mr Durrell, I've been to your place now several times and I think it's marvellous,' he said. 'I think the animals are in wonderful condition, but I think your reptile house stinks.'

I agreed, but had to explain that the converted garage was all we could afford.

The sleek and handsome Telfair's skink, a lizard only found on the tiny volcanic Round island.

'You find the money,' I said jokingly, 'and I'll build you the finest reptile house in the world.'

He looked at me pensively for a moment, and then he went off and that was the last I thought of it. But at the end of the conference he came to me once again:

'Mr Durrell, were you serious when you said that if I found you the money that you'd build the finest reptile house in the world?' he asked.

'I certainly was,' I said. 'Why?'

'Well, *um*, among my other qualifications, I, *um*, happen to be an eccentric millionaire,' he said.

For a moment, I stared at him disbelievingly, then:

'Step into my office,' I said, faintly.

So that is how we got what must be one of the finest reptile houses in the world, if not the finest, and it is here that we have had some spectacular successes. Among the rarest of these are three species which are found only on Round Island, a minute carunculated bit of volcanic tuff fourteen miles off the Mauritian coast. Two are lizards, the sleek, handsome Telfair's skink and the dark, soft-skinned, cat-eyed Guenther's gecko. The third is a snake, the Round Island

Members of the expedition
and the Mauritian crew set up
a crane on Round island to
ferry both humans and equipment from the anchored boat
over razor-sharp rocks.

Round Island, fourteen miles
off the Mauritian coast,
showing severe erosion.

Years of erosion have turned
Round Island into a jumble of
deep pleats and scallops.

boa, which presents problems to both zoogeographers and taxonomists. How did a boa-like snake (when boas are New World snakes) come to evolve on a tiny speck of land in the Indian Ocean? John and I had collected colonies of all three species on previous trips to the Mascarenes and all have successfully bred. (As a matter of fact, as I was writing this chapter I received the news that our Round Island boa's eggs had hatched out, the first time this species has been bred in captivity and a great herpetological and conservation triumph.) So, on this trip, we were anxious to revisit Round Island to try to get more specimens of each species to increase our gene pool.

The Mauritian authorities offered us their full co-operation and so we found ourselves, late one morning, riding blue, glittering waves, just off the island, in six fathoms of beautifully transparent water. Our small boat's anchor held us in position while John Hartley, accompanied by three of the burly policemen the Mauritian Government had generously assigned to help us with our equipment, swam ashore towing lines to set up a small crane we would use to get our supplies and equipment (and ourselves) ashore. I watched rather apprehensively as John bobbed along in the water, because getting ashore in that swell can be dangerous, for the waves can dash you against the razor-sharp rocks. Lee was too excited to worry about the risks to anyone, including herself.

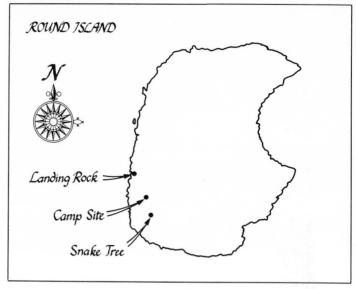

John scrambled enthusiastically ashore with the policemen and they were all soon busy lashing together the landing lines. Even with the ropes and the help of the Mauritian policemen, landing on Round Island was more exciting than I felt was strictly desirable for one of my ripening vintage and avoirdupois. Still, the arrangement was a considerable improvement over the way it had been done in the past. There is only one landing site on the entire 370-acre island and it consists merely of a large flat rock where someone long ago attached a couple of iron rings to which lines can be made fast. The last time I visited the island the landing drill consisted of leaping from the gunwales of the boat's dinghy as it rose and fell on the polished swells, and coming down with an undignified crash on the slippery rock. This time you were swung ashore by the crane while sitting in a loop of rope. I must say it made me feel like an elderly Peter Pan. Lee, on the other hand, looking very decorative in a large sun-hat, thoroughly enjoyed the experience.

Once the boat has left and you are marooned with your supplies and equipment, you then discover that landing was the easy part. Our first objective was the picnic tree, a large pandanus that spread its fan-like leaves about 250 feet above us, at the top of the escarpment, and so we loaded ourselves down with our paraphernalia and began the climb. Centuries of erosion of the volcanic tuff have turned the island landscape into a jumble of deep pleats and scallops, and

although the surface appears smooth, when you step on it the thin crust is likely to crumble and slip away under your feet. The heat is intense, even in the early morning, and the air is heavy with salt. By mid-afternoon the rock is often hot enough to literally fry eggs on. By the time we had reached the top of the cliff, panting and bathed in sweat, we were grateful for the little pools of shade offered by the pandanus.

At one time all of the lower slopes of the island were covered with thick palm forest, and the higher parts were forested in ebony and other hardwoods. But in the early nineteenth century rabbits and goats were introduced and they have created a desert. Goats in particular go straight through a forest eating everything on the ground, including seedlings (without which the forest cannot renew itself) and even climbing up the trees as skilfully as monkeys in their pursuit of the last leaf. Fortunately, rats were not introduced, for if they had been it would have been the end of the reptile fauna.

The Government of Mauritius has turned Round Island into a nature preserve, we hope just in time to save what remains of the two species of lizard, two species of snake and two species of palm tree that have evolved on this tiny speck of land and that exist nowhere else in the world. The goats have finally been eliminated, so there is some hope that, in time, the forest may make a come-back, if one can get the rabbits under control.

Once thickly forested with palm trees and hardwoods, the island is now a desert with only a few species of palm tree left.

Lying under a constant intense heat, the thin crust of ground covering Round island crumbles away easily under-foot.

A gecko making a gravity-defying vertical ascent.

No sooner had we stretched ourselves thankfully in the shade of the pandanus than out from every nook and cranny in the rocks emerged a host of the large, iridescent Telfair's skinks. They were charmingly tame and poked their noses into everything, peering at us enquiringly with large, intelligent eyes. They are completely fearless because they have no natural predators: they are right at the top of the food chain on the island, and they pursue all the smaller lizards and eat them if they can. It seems to me an enormous privilege to have such a reptile climb up onto my lap and eat the morsels of food I offer it, particularly when you think that it has come down from the age of the dinosaurs. However, Lee decided it was a somewhat doubtful privilege when a very large Telfair's who was sitting in her lap seized her finger instead of the bit of banana she was offering him. They have powerful jaws and it was some time before we could staunch the blood.

'Never mind,' I consoled her, tying a handkerchief round her finger. 'Just think, you're probably the first female doctor he's ever bitten. What a distinction.'

'Thank you,' she said, witheringly. 'I shall treat with caution in future all the things you tell me are tame.'

But as they drank Coca-Cola and shared our sandwiches it was frightening to realise that there are so few of them left that one really bad cyclone could make these lovely, endearing creatures vanish forever.

The expedition camps out on Round island.

We set up camp under a scattering of palm trees at the edge of a small valley. It was in fact close to the area where I had camped on my previous visits. Camping had always been an exhilarating if somewhat hazardous experience on Round Island. On my first trip for example, the shearwaters were nesting in their hundreds in holes underneath our tent. As soon as darkness fell the babies all started shouting and honking to one another in a cacophonous underground chorus. Then they emerged and started not only invading the tent (which they doubtless thought was a lovely outsize burrow) but also climbing to the ridge and sliding down the slopes of the tent, as if it were a sort of ski slope. The sound of their claws scraping on the canvas was as conducive to sleep as a knife squeaking on a plate.

I had warned Lee about the possibility of being kept awake by baby birds and she, in her enthusiasm, thought it would be very amusing. However, it turned out that — to my relief — the shearwater breeding season was just over, and so I looked forward to an uninterrupted night's sleep without strong-smelling baby shearwaters trying to climb into my bed or honk loudly in my ear. But it was not to be, for the moment the sun sank there appeared from nowhere literally hundreds of thousands of tiny dark moths each about three-sixteenths of an inch long. They found our tent and our persons absolutely irresistible. We were, in their opinion, the most delectable things that they had encountered in their small lives. Myriads of them gathered to make the most of us. Within minutes the tent was thick with them, the canvas walls a black, moving, fluttering mass. In desperation, in spite of the heat, we closed the tent flaps, but it was no use for the moths were small enough to find their way through the tiniest chink. Rather than spend the night locked in with a seething mass of moths, we took our blankets out onto the rocks; but here it was just as bad. We were covered with thousands of them and they crawled all over us, into our hair, our eyes, up our noses, into our ears. You could kill five hundred with a slap, but immediately another five hundred took their place.

'Didn't you say you once used to collect moths?' asked Lee, spitting out a mouthful.

'Yes,' I said, irritably. 'I used to be quite fond of the damn things, but after this, give me baby shearwaters every time.'

'Well, at least you didn't get shearwaters up your nose,' said Lee.

'No, I suppose that could be called a consolation of some sort,' I observed.

'What interesting lives we naturalists lead,' said Lee, expectorating another brigade of lepidoptera, 'so romantic, so interesting.'

We were thankful to see the dawn stain the sky tangerine, against which the palm trees stood in black silhouette, while around them hung a grey mist of moths flying off to their daytime resting places.

By noon the following day we had captured our quota of Telfair's skinks, having hiked as far away from the picnic tree as we could. We had collected our first batch near the tree last time and so we wanted to make sure our new additions were from a different area. It *is* possible to catch the Telfair's by hand, but on Round Island that can be an exhausting and sometimes dangerous proposition, because of the heat and uncertain footing. I speak from bitter experience when I say that it is no fun at all sliding pell-mell down those rocky gorges on your backside, using your elbows for brakes—and I have scars to prove it. So what we did was to snare them in fine nylon nooses attached to the ends of long bamboo poles. Once you have slowly and gently slipped the noose over the head and forelegs, you jerk it tight for long enough to grab the skink and drop it in a cloth collecting bag, where it is quite comfortable until you can get it back to the base camp and put it in a proper cage.

Locating and capturing the other species we were after, the Guenther's gecko, was a more difficult proposition. There are only about a hundred of them left in the wild state and their marvellous camouflage makes them hard to spot. They are adapted to live in the palm trees and their velvety skin is a mottled grey and chocolate that looks just like lichen, or some discoloration on the tree bark; and with the little suction pads they have on their toes, they can scuttle up and down the tree trunks like a fly on a window-pane. However, in spite of the difficulties, by the time the day was out we had a number of fat, healthy specimens of both sexes to add to our breeding stock back on Jersey.

The biggest triumph of the day, though, was John's. We had spent a long, hot and prickly time investigat-

Over one hundred of the endangered Telfair's skinks have been bred in captivity since 1976.

ing the low-growing clumps of palms which is where
one of the species of Round Island boa likes to hang
out. It is tedious and painstaking work for, first of all,
as there are only some seventy specimens left they are
not what one would describe as common. Secondly,
they merge beautifully with their surroundings and
generally stay very still, so they are hard to see. Lee,
John and I were just searching what must have been
our hundredth palm tree apiece, when John uttered a
yell of triumph and started dancing about, waving his
arms, looking like an exceptionally lanky crane doing a
mating dance.

'Quickly, quickly!' he yelled, 'I found one.'

Lee and I ran to join him and surrounded the palm
in case the snake tried to make a break for it. Once sure
it could not escape, John inserted a long arm into the
palm leaves and caught it skilfully round the neck.
Then I carefully unravelled its body with Lee's help
and we soon had it disentangled from its lair. It was the
biggest one we had caught to date and, to our delight,
a female, which is just what we needed.

'Isn't she a beauty,' crowed John with joy. 'A positive
Pythagoras.'

'What's a positive Pythagoras?' asked Lee, puzzled;
and I explained.

It was in the days when we still had our reptiles in
Jersey living in the converted garage and the creatures
had to be taken out of their cages so that their homes
could be cleaned every week. Among our specimens
we had a huge, beautiful but bad-tempered python
called Pythagoras, some twelve feet long. He had to be
extracted from his cage and incarcerated in a big laun-
dry basket while cleaning progressed. John, who was
in charge of the reptiles then, had been told never to
attempt this on his own, for Pythagoras was dangerous. One morning, however, John foolhardily tried to
do it on his own. I happened to pass the reptile house
and heard calls for help. Going in, I found John wound

John Hartley examines the Round island boa he has just captured.

round from head to foot, like a maypole, by Pythagoras's coils. I grabbed the python's tail and started to unwind him, but as fast as I did so he wound round me, until John and I were completely tangled up in the reptile's coils. In the end we *both* had to call for help until another member of the staff came to our rescue, an embarrassing moment for both of us.

It's frustrating having to leave a place like Round Island after only a couple of days, for you know that if you had six weeks or so you could get down to doing some really sensible ecological work and could learn so much about the island's flora and fauna. But we had had very good luck, and we had the satisfaction of knowing the island's reptiles were a little safer now than they had been before we arrived. The beauty of trying to save Round Island is in the fact that we don't have to stop *man* from doing anything. In practically every other place we have worked, saving endangered species involves getting someone to stop digging or stop building or stop cutting down trees and so on. But on Round Island, man did his damage a hundred and eighty-odd years ago in however long it took him to open a few boxes and let loose the rabbits and goats. The goats are gone now, and one day the rabbits will be, too, we hope. As things stand now, you can see evidence of the havoc these creatures wreak everywhere you look: their shallow burrows dug where they promote maximum erosion; the tops of the palm seedlings nipped off; the pruning and stunting of the patches of pretty convolvulus-type ground cover that is trying valiantly but forlornly to hold the soil together against the onslaught of wind and rain.

But once we can stop the rot, to a very great extent this dying island can help save itself, through natural regeneration. And meanwhile we will be breeding the skinks and geckos and the boas, getting ready to reintroduce them into their natural habitat some time in the future. But ideally, what would make us all happiest, strangely enough, would be to close down our breeding colonies because the island was safe and captive breeding was no longer necessary to help these unique reptiles.

The Bat
Colony of
Rodrigues

The great blue expanse of the Indian Ocean in which the Mascarenes lie scattered is the breeding ground for cyclones. Here they hatch and, bearing deceptively demure and feminine names, they prowl ferociously, ready to suddenly turn and run screaming at an island when least expected, churning the waves to froth-covered monsters, whipping the land with winds like huge solid fists that tear and uproot trees and play with houses as though they were constructed of cardboard. Apart from the damage to human life and to property, these cyclones are enormously detrimental to the flora and fauna of the islands, and particularly dangerous for those species whose numbers are few and whose food supply is already limited. The duration of a cyclone is important too, for such things as birds and bats cannot fly in those gargantuan gusts of wind and so they cannot feed and in the momentary lulls when the wind dies to a whisper they find the trees stripped of leaves and fruit and insects blown away like chaff. Of the many cyclones that have hit the Mascarenes in the last decade they all, without exception, seem to have singled out the island of Rodrigues to vent their wrath on. In 1968, for example, one by the seductive name of *Monique* leapt on the island and lashed it with winds of up to 170 miles an hour.

Because of habitat destruction by man and the repeated attention of cyclones, there were two species of creature found in Rodrigues which urgently needed help. One was the delightful and delicate little Rodrigues fody, a small yellow, orange and black bird which was, a hundred or so years ago, very common on the island. But with the steady disappearance of its habitat, combined with the introduction of the much tougher and more adaptable Malagasy fody, who competes for the meagre food supply, this attractive little bird was in dire straits. Then came the diabolical *Monique*, and when she — cat-like — had finished

A group of endearing little Rodrigues fruit-bats, the rarest bats in the world.

playing with the island and had passed on screaming into the ocean, there were only six pairs of fody left alive, only twelve small, fragile birds left to continue the species. It seemed touch and go but then the fody had some luck. The various cyclones, for a few years, left the island alone. During this time of peace the little bird managed to build its numbers up to over one hundred pairs. This was wonderful but we all wondered what would happen when the next cyclone struck. Was it not possible that it might be even more devastating than *Monique*? As a precautionary measure the Mauritian Government decided to let us take six pairs back to Jersey to set up a captive breeding colony. Now, on our return two years later, the wild population had had another period of cyclonic attention and so we were ánxious to visit the island and see how they had stood up to this pressure.

The other species on the island that gave cause for concern was the lovely little fruit-bat, which is probably the rarest bat in the world. In 1976, we estimated that the total world population was between 120 and 130 specimens, and so—again as a precautionary measure—the Mauritian Government asked us to catch a sufficient number to start two breeding colonies, one in Jersey and one in the aviaries at Black River. Our Jersey colony had flourished and had grown from the original ten specimens to over thirty, but nevertheless we felt it would be helpful to our breeding success to obtain one or two more specimens on this visit to extend our gene pool.

The entire island of Rodrigues is surrounded by a vast coral reef, exposed for miles at low tide.

Landing at the tiny airport of Rodrigues.

Rodrigues lies 360 miles from Mauritius and the flight to its tiny airport takes you over the vast blue carpet of the Indian Ocean. As you watch the brilliant blue expanse below it reminds you vividly of how much of the world is covered by water. After one hour's flying you can just discern a faint brown smudge on the horizon which is the island, and as you get closer, you can see the brown eroded landscape, the tiny, pathetic pockets of green in the valleys and the whole island encircled by a vast reef on which the waves break continuously in a crumple of foam like a giant lace cuff protecting the island.

Rodrigues now seems so desiccated, so dry, so lacking in forest that it is hard to think that when it was first settled by a group of nine Huguenots, escaping from persecution in France in 1691, they christened the settlement Eden because of the rich bounty the island offered. Among these first settlers was one François Leguat, an astute observer, and it is from his written descriptions of the island as they found it that allow us to imagine what a magical place it must have been.

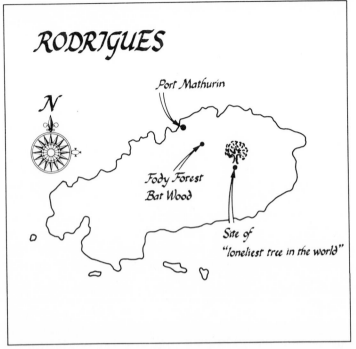

The island of Rodrigues, lying 360 miles across the Indian Ocean from Mauritius.

To begin with the island was thickly forested with hundreds of species of tree and shrub, so when the seeds the settlers had so carefully brought from France refused to grow it scarcely mattered, for nature on this paradise was rich and bountiful. Fruit and vegetables grew everywhere in profusion. The settlers made wine and spirits from the palm trees. The vast, frothy apron of the reef, exposed for miles at low tide, teemed with thousands of fish, oysters, lobsters and crabs. In the lagoons, feeding on the seaweeds, were herds of massive, placid and easily killed dugong, the huge marine mammal rather like a seal, whose flesh was delicious and whose carcass yielded valuable oil. Nor was the interior of the island any the less bountiful. Bird life was abundant and, having no enemies, the birds were tame and easy to kill. Especially easy in this respect was a turkey-sized flightless bird called the solitaire, which like the dodo was soon to become extinct. The island was also full of a species of giant tortoise, each one the size of a large armchair, that ambled in their thousands through the forests. So common were these huge reptiles that Leguat wrote, 'Sometimes you can see two or three thousand of them in a flock, so that you may go a hundred paces on their backs without setting foot to the ground.'

Alas, the arrival of the settlers was the death knell for this wonderful island. The settlers themselves did not stay long for, in spite of the richness of the island, the lack of feminine companionship drove them to Mauritius. But the tales they told of their Eden soon had ships calling at Rodrigues, and, as man has always done, the island was raped ruthlessly and unmercifully. The forests were felled for timber. The birds and the dugongs were harried to extinction, as were the tortoises. Ships would call in and take thousands of tortoises on board as living meat supplies, such as a modern vessel may take on tinned hams. Very shortly the animal life dwindled and was gone, the forest vanished and this 'Garden of Eden' lay an eroded husk after the locust-like attack of man. Thus in three hundred years man, through thoughtless greed, had turned a rich and beautiful place into what it is today, almost a desert, the home of some 35,000 people who eke out a marginal existence as fishermen or small farmers and who carry out a desultory trade with Mauritius.

Although, ecologically speaking, Rodrigues may be considered a disaster area, it has all the charm of a small, remote and sunlit island, inhabited by gentle, friendly people. We drove into Port Mathurin, the

Native fishermen on Rodrigues hauling in their daily catch.

pocket handkerchief-sized capital, and then up the hill to the long, low, slightly ramshackle building with broad verandahs looking out over the blue sea that is Rodrigues's one and only hotel. Here we unpacked our gear and then, taking the Forestry Department's Land-Rover, we drove up for a reconnaissance to the place where the bat colony lived, the picturesquely named Cascade Pigeon.

Here, lying on the sides of a deep valley, was one of the last remnants of forest in Rodrigues. It was not very tall or very dense, but in the middle of it, on one of the flanks of the valley, grew a small grove of old and luxuriant mango trees. It was in the deep shade of their glossy green leaves that the Rodrigues fruit-bat had its home and its last stand against extinction. At first glance through the binoculars the uninitiated might be pardoned for thinking that the mangoes were possessed of a crop of strange, wind-fluttered, furry, chocolate-coloured fruit. But as the bats yawn and stretch their wings the illusion is dispelled. Now you can see that with their leathery dark wings and their fur that ranges from deep fox-red to the colour of spun gold, they look like some wonderful miniature flying teddy bears, a resemblance that is helped by their bear-like little faces with button noses and round, bright eyes.

Most people have a fear of bats that is quite irrational, presumably to a large extent helped by the tales of Count Dracula and his ilk. But in reality they are charming, intelligent little creatures, the only mammals possessed of true flight, and to see them at Cascade Pigeon, as they lazily wheeled and flapped their way from tree to tree, was to realise how extraordinary and graceful an adaptation it is.

Fruit-bats, unlike their useful insect-eating relatives, are not equipped with built-in sonar. They have to detect their food by their acute sense of smell. In order to catch them we planned to use, as we had used

The Rodrigues fruit-bat, threatened with extinction, has a wild population estimated in 1979 at a mere 70 specimens.

on our previous trip to Rodrigues, a variety of fruits brought over from Mauritius (there were no such luxuries in poor, desiccated Rodrigues). In our extensive array of bananas, mangoes, guavas and the like was a malevolent fruit known as a jackfruit. This green, warty, watermelon-sized fruit is considered by both some human beings and all fruit-bats to be a rare delicacy, and it is difficult, if not impossible, to imagine why. Its smell is sweet, sickly, cloying and clinging, and is a happy cross between an open grave of some years' standing and a thoroughly blocked-up sewer. We kept this ghastly fruit tightly swaddled in plastic, but even so the scent — if that is not too enthusiastic a word — leaked out and permeated everything. At the airport in Mauritius people coughed furtively and eyed us with suspicion. Within minutes the interior of the plane reeked of jackfruit to the consternation of the other passengers. Arriving in Rodrigues we and all our equipment smelt of nothing but the all-pervading jackfruit. Even Lee, in spite of lavish applications of Eau de Cologne, gave off an almost tangible shimmer of effluvium and put a grave strain on our marriage.

Our plan was to hoist all the fruit aloft in a clearing near the bat colony and then surround it with mist nets into which (as had happened last time) the bats would blunder in search of the bait. We finished the trap by nightfall just when the bats, with much squeaking and chattering and wing-flapping, were making ready to fly off down the valley in search of food. Then we concealed ourselves in the bushes and waited, for you cannot simply leave a trap like this and return in the morning after a refreshing night's sleep. You would probably find any bats you had caught had damaged themselves with their struggles to get free and some might even have strangled themselves. You have to stay all night by your nets ready to cut the little bats loose as they are caught. So we settled down, the jackfruit reeking like a charnel-house thirty feet above

A colony of bats hang like strange fruit from the trees in the forest.

us, to while away the time with what appeared to be the entire mosquito population of Rodrigues.

Collecting wild animals is, to say the least of it, unpredictable. You may strike lucky straight away, or you may hunt the forest for days fruitlessly, only to find that a maid has caught you the animal you want under your bed in the hotel. This occasion was one of the frustrating examples. Three tiring, mosquito-ridden nights later, all we had caught was one bat—a male, moreover, which was useless to us. But the reason that the bats were ignoring our odoriferous fruit bait was, we thought, a good one. In the last few years the island had received an unprecedented rain-fall, and in consequence what was left of the forest had flourished and expanded marginally so that the bats now had a wider variety of feeding areas. From a conservation point of view this was, of course, excel-lent news, but it was a little difficult to be too enthusi-astic at three o'clock in the morning when you were sharing your red corpuscles with a lot of voracious mosquitoes.

So we failed with the bats. But we were more suc-cessful with our second task, which was to try to do a census of the fody to see how its numbers were faring. It was here that Lee came into her own, for, as I have explained, she had spent two years in Madagascar studying animal communication, which is the scien-tific description of how animals talk to one another. We now know that most animals use sound in a much more complex way than we believed. Take bird song, for example. At one time people thought that birds sang because they were happy, say, or because their wife had just laid another egg. We have now discov-ered that song and the other noises animals make have a wide variety of meanings. In the case of bird song, what the bird is really doing is putting up vocal 'Private Property' signs, for other cock birds hearing the song know that this piece of territory has been staked out

The Rodrigues fruit bat.

and claimed by the singing owner. By using the bird's territorial instincts against itself, as it were, one can find out a lot about numbers and territory. It works like this. Lee, with cunning and patience, obtained a recording of a cock fody singing his territorial song.

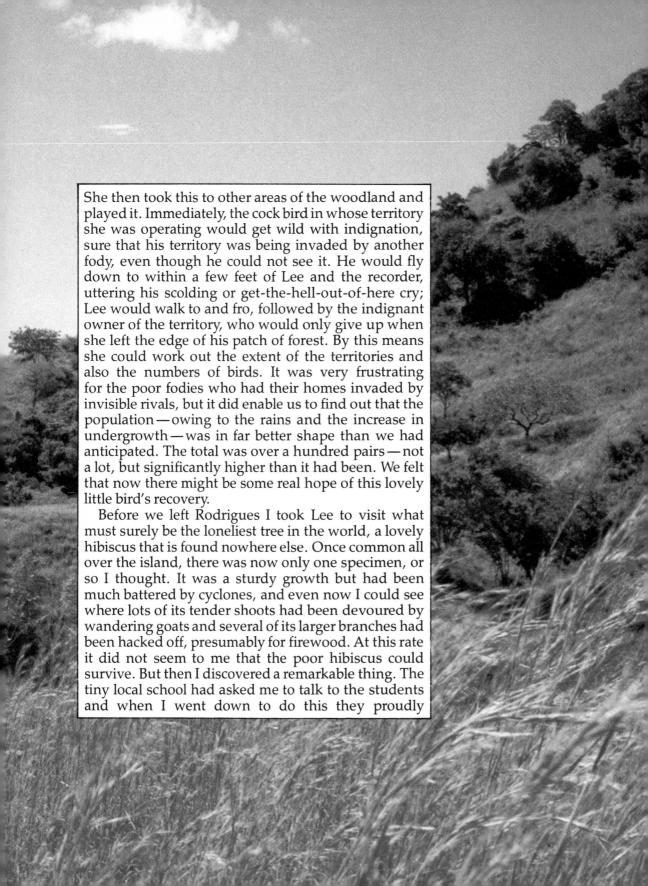

She then took this to other areas of the woodland and played it. Immediately, the cock bird in whose territory she was operating would get wild with indignation, sure that his territory was being invaded by another fody, even though he could not see it. He would fly down to within a few feet of Lee and the recorder, uttering his scolding or get-the-hell-out-of-here cry; Lee would walk to and fro, followed by the indignant owner of the territory, who would only give up when she left the edge of his patch of forest. By this means she could work out the extent of the territories and also the numbers of birds. It was very frustrating for the poor fodies who had their homes invaded by invisible rivals, but it did enable us to find out that the population—owing to the rains and the increase in undergrowth—was in far better shape than we had anticipated. The total was over a hundred pairs—not a lot, but significantly higher than it had been. We felt that now there might be some real hope of this lovely little bird's recovery.

Before we left Rodrigues I took Lee to visit what must surely be the loneliest tree in the world, a lovely hibiscus that is found nowhere else. Once common all over the island, there was now only one specimen, or so I thought. It was a sturdy growth but had been much battered by cyclones, and even now I could see where lots of its tender shoots had been devoured by wandering goats and several of its larger branches had been hacked off, presumably for firewood. At this rate it did not seem to me that the poor hibiscus could survive. But then I discovered a remarkable thing. The tiny local school had asked me to talk to the students and when I went down to do this they proudly

A tiny, but sturdy, baby hibiscus tree, a cutting taken from its lonely parent in the hopes of saving this rare species of Rodrigues flora.

One of a hundred pairs of the beautiful little Rodrigues fody counted by the expedition and now making a comeback from the edge of extinction.

showed me (to my astonishment) a sturdy baby hibiscus in a pot. Apparently, realising the rarity of the shrub, the local school had adopted it and taken several cuttings. Some had been sent to Kew Gardens, where, unfortunately, they failed to live; but this one cutting grew and prospered. It was about a foot high when I saw it. The school intends to take more cuttings in the hope that others may thrive and the hibiscus may once again become as common as it had been. Goodness knows, Rodrigues needs every green thing it can save, so we hope the hibiscus will survive under the care of the children.

The Treasure
Island of
Madagascar

The plane flew steadily through the brilliant blue sky while Madagascar, the world's fourth largest island and probably biologically the world's most important island, started to unroll thousands of feet below us. Soon the lush rim of eastern rain forests, a complex mat of greens and reds and purples, gave way to the bare uplands. Here you could see the eroded landscape, great areas wrinkled as a tortoise skin and almost blood-red in colour, with here and there pockets of jade-green grass or small patches of forest in the valleys. In the forested rim of the island I knew we should find a breath-taking collection of creatures and plants, for Madagascar, from the zoologist's and botanist's point of view, is a treasure-house of unique forms of life. This is the home of the incredible lemurs and the hunting grounds of strange mongoose-like predators found nowhere else. Here have evolved over forty-five kinds of chameleon, and whereas Africa can boast of one species of baobab tree, Madagascar has nine. There are strange birds, mammals, reptiles, insects and plants which are all found nowhere else but in this living museum. How all these creatures came to be here is an amazing story in itself.

For many years zoologists were puzzled by the distribution of animals all over the world in what appeared to be a rather haphazard, sporadic and curious manner. Why, for example, were there elephants in Africa and India but not in Australia? Conversely, why were there kangaroos in Australia but not in Africa? For many years this remained a riddle, but then, comparatively recently, new evidence was found to confirm an idea the zoologists had had, the notion of continental drift.

We know now that since life started to evolve on earth the earth's geography has been evolving as well. It is still imperceptibly changing, with the great land masses drifting further apart in some places and closer together in others. Over millions of years the earth has been warped and changed by immense volcanic forces and the pressure of the seas, and the continents, like gigantic granite rafts, floated to and fro over the earth's cloak of dense but liquid basalt. At one point in history all the southern land masses were huddled together in one great conglomeration called Gondwanaland, and so both plants and animal forms could migrate freely over this huge continent. But then it started to split up like a jigsaw puzzle, forming southern Asia, South America, Africa and Australia. As they drifted away from each other they carried with them their cargoes of animals and plants, and so these evolved along their own lines without contact with the other continental 'rafts'.

About a hundred million years ago, a great leaf-shaped land mass broke away from east Africa and floated off into the Indian Ocean to become Madagascar. The bulk of its wonderful array of plant and animal life is descended from African forms of this ancient era. But as recently as sixty million years ago the island was still within 'rafting' distance of Africa, and so the early forms of monkey — the prosimians — could be carried across from continental Africa on massive tree trunks uprooted by floods, pushed out into the ocean and tide-propelled to Madagascar's shore. The rafts carried other living cargoes — seeds, spores, reptiles, insects and other forms of mammal. So the wonderful thing about Madagascar is that its creatures go directly back to Gondwana and the time of the earliest primates. For millions of years, unmolested by man, the animal and plant life of Madagascar evolved into a fantastic array of lemurs, showing us alternative evolutionary pathways to those of our earliest African ancestors, which range from the great black-and-white indri, the size of a six-year-old child, to the delicate, big-eyed mouse lemur, three of which would fit into a teacup. There were also other extraordinary beasts but these began to vanish with the coming of man: ten species of large lemur, one that grew to the size of a calf; giant tortoises and twenty-four-foot crocodiles; pygmy hippos lolling in the swamps; and, haunting the forests, the *Aepyornis* or elephant bird, the heaviest bird ever, clumping through the under- growth on elephantine feet. Looking like a magnified ostrich standing ten feet high, this fantastic bird laid eggs that could hold two and a half gallons and could have (and probably did) provide an omelette for up to seventy-two people. It was definitely not the sort of egg you find in a supermarket. It is thought that Sinbad's famous Roc, which could soar away carrying elephants in its claws, was probably based on *Aepyornis*.

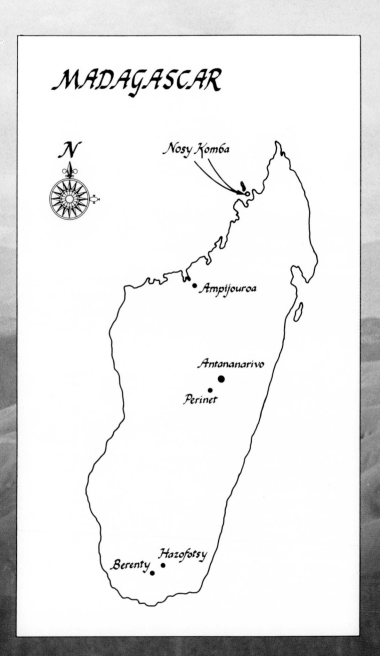

Not only did all these creatures become extinct with the coming of man, but the habitat of the survivors now started to change under the pressures from *Homo sapiens*. As usual the felling of the forest to create farmland was the beginning, and then the grasslands thus created were burnt to provide sweet young shoots for zebu. A pall of smoke hung and still, at certain times of the year, hangs over Madagascar. The island chokes in this shroud of smoke; the red earth, no longer protected by the leafy overcoat of forest, is washed away. This dribbles into the rivers, which run red like huge arteries, and then the earth is carried out to the sea in a giant red mantle. This is Madagascar, bleeding to death from self-inflicted wounds. The slash-and-burn agriculture, which did not matter when the population was small and the forest had a chance to regenerate, is still practised today by an ever-increasing population numbering nearly ten million people. The forests are under pressure, too, from the gigantic herds of zebu which graze indiscriminately, even in areas designated as reserves.

Ecologically speaking, man is killing Madagascar, and so himself, as he is doing in so many parts of the world. However, many Malagasy are fully aware of their remarkable and valuable heritage and are trying their best to do something to save it. There are excellent biologists, foresters, agronomists and educators in Madagascar, but their projects need financial support and their ranks need reinforcements.

Over the past few years in Jersey we have started several breeding groups of Malagasy fauna, and have met with considerable success. Among the smaller creatures are some strange little insectivores known as tenrecs. These little animals — of which there are many different species — resemble European hedgehogs, but instead of rolling into a ball when threatened, they merely pull down the prickly skin of the head over their noses in a ferocious scowl. There is one species we had, the streaked tenrec, which has black and white spines in varying lengths arranged in stripes in its pale-yellowish fur. These spines, it has been discovered, not only act as a defence mechanism, but are used by the mother as a means of communication with her generally large litter of babies, enchanting little things that, when newly born look like a brood of spiky bumble-bees. As they are numerous and agile the mother keeps track of them by constantly stridulating the spines on her back, which produces a shrill, cricket-like noise that is partly supersonic and to which the young reply, and thus the harassed mother can keep tabs on her family. Tenrecs feed on a wide variety of insects, as well as slugs, snails and worms, fulfilling in Madagascar the role played by shrews, hedgehogs and moles in Europe.

We had considerable success breeding the pygmy hedgehog tenrec. The reason we took so much trouble over a common species is that, by learning to breed them successfully we were evolving techniques which would stand us in good stead when we attempted to build up colonies of the rarer and more endangered species.

A lapful of tenrecs.

Feeding the Ring-tail lemur colony in Jersey.

A ring-tailed lemur shows off its uniquely coloured fur coat and tail.

Among our collection of lemurs in Jersey, one of the commonest, but one of the most attractive, is the ring-tailed lemur, a wonderful creature that, in its beautifully marked fur of black, white, ash-grey and a touch of rufous, and with its long black-and-white-ringed tail, looks as though it's been designed by a very famous, very chic, very expensive and probably very gay interior decorator. Their whole artistically laid out colour scheme is rounded off by the fact that they have large, round, tangerine-coloured eyes.

The rarer species are the brown lemurs, rather leggy, svelte creatures with fur that ranges from chocolate brown, through cinnamon to *café au lait*. They are not nearly so startling to look at as the ringtails, their coloration being more blurred and subtle, but they are most attractive, agile creatures and have bred well with us.

A group of the curious spiky little insectivore known as the streaked tenrec.

Madagascar bleeds: the island's earth is washed away to the sea through artery-like rivers.

But undoubtedly the rarest and the most spectacular of our lemurs are the huge, woolly ruffed lemurs, as big as a medium-sized dog. They can be.described as the giant panda of the lemur world, for their thick fur is patterned with black and white and touches of bright orange here and there. They have very large, protuberant, straw-coloured eyes with a wild expression, like that of a madman surveying with perpetual astonishment the activities of a sane world. These large, bouncing, handsome creatures are my favourite among our Malagasy collection. One of the things I like best about them is that not only are they spectacular to look at, but their songs have to be heard to be believed. It is difficult always to see what sets them off, but generally two or three times during the day or in the early morning one will start a series of cries that are harsh, penetrating and very loud, like a cross between a roar and a bark. The others all join in at intervals, like a part song, until finally you have the full troop singing, and a deafening, spine-chilling chorus it is. The more nervous of our house guests have been known to drop a cup of scalding tea into their laps when first hearing the ruffed lemurs start to sing. One rather desperate publisher had to be revived with a whisky at seven in the morning, so great was the shock to his nerves, for he thought our snow leopards had escaped. As the male had spent the afternoon stalking my friend along the wire of the cage, he naturally assumed that he would be first on the menu should this beautiful cat get loose.

A rare and beautiful woolly ruffed lemur gazes out in wonder from its leafy bower.

A lemur pauses to listen to its singing mates.

A baby ringtail lemur clings to its mother.

The golden stare of a pensive lemur.

Antananarivo, the capital of Madagascar, is a colourful, bustling and lovely city, with mud houses of curious architecture in pale-brown, fawn and pinkish tones with multicoloured shutters, which climb over the hills like a town of toy bricks and stand tessellated against the blue sky. Through the centre runs the broad, tree-lined boulevard, L'Avenue de l'Indépendance, which once a week is transformed by the great Zoma market. Luckily the market coincided with our arrival, and the stalls were already set out along the broad pavements of the boulevard, each guarded from the sun by white canvas umbrellas. We adore markets of any sort and the Zoma is probably one of the most exotic markets I have seen anywhere in the world. As we wandered happily through the gay, jostling throngs, who wore bright clothes and multicoloured straw hats, we admired the extraordinary array of goods for sale. Here were great baskets laden with chick peas, dried corn, couscous, dried beans and rice. Nearby were flocks of white turkeys with scarlet faces; groups of ducks, their feet tied, a dish of water near each group; hundreds of chickens of a bewildering pageant of colours. There were giant baskets of eggs, of apples, pineapples, mangoes, oranges and other fruits. There were huge carved wooden bedsteads, baskets of raffia, of rope, of cane; huge tin trunks, gaily painted; bags and wallets and suitcases fashioned of thick pungent leather. There were cotton garments embroidered with gay flowers; there were handkerchiefs and trousers and rope-soled sandals. There were huge wall-hangings of thick, crude, parchment-like paper into which had been carefully embedded dried pressed flowers in lovely pastel shades. There were, unfortunately, boxes of butterflies and stuffed chameleons, and jewel-cases and cigarette-cases of turtle- and tortoise-shell. And there were the local precious and semi-precious stones and crystals glittering in piles like a king's ransom. It was a splendid

market, filled with happy smiling people, and the
whole thing redolent of a hundred fruits and flowers
and animals. Climbing the broad steps that led to the
upper part of town, we looked back at the market
which, with its white umbrellas and its exotic, colourful merchandise, looked like a huge mushroom bed
scattered with multicoloured confetti. One would
always long to return to Madagascar, I thought, if only
to revisit the spectacular Zoma.

The colourful native Zoma
market in Antananarivo, capital of Madagascar.

It was at this point in Antananarivo, while we were starting to plan our movements, that our guardian angel appeared in the shape of Professor Roland Albignac, an old friend of ours and one who had worked in Madagascar for years. I must say that, with his jaunty black beard, his bronzed face, eagle nose and bright blue eyes, he looked more Mephistophelian than angelic, but our guardian angel he became. We sat at a tiny table on the pavement outside the hotel, surrounded by people trying to sell us everything from silver bracelets and hand-painted picture postcards to multicoloured straw hats. Over refreshing beer, I outlined the various places we wanted to visit and the animals we wanted to film. Roland listened carefully.

'Well,' I said, when I had finished. 'What d'you think, Roland?'

The expedition's guardian angel in Madagascar: Professor 'Pas de Problème' Roland Albignac.

It was then that Roland uttered his favourite phrase which was to become his nickname and the expedition's watchword.

'Pas de problème,' he said, shrugging and giving us his Mephistophelian grin. So Professor Pas de Problème he became forthwith and, indeed, with his wonderful help there *were* no problems.

The Dance
of the
Lemurs

Our first expedition out of Antananarivo was to fly right down to the south of the island to Fort Dauphin, now called Taolañaro. This is a pretty, quiet little port, surrounded by beautiful, pale, straw-coloured beaches which embrace the warm blue sea. Here we paused only long enough to enjoy some of the fabulous oysters and lobsters which abound, and then we headed for our goal which was the reserve at Berenty, lying some fifty miles to the west of the port.

Berenty, with its colonies of ring-tailed lemurs, has the distinction of being the best-studied area in Madagascar. The reserve is the brain-child of Monsieur Jean DeHeaulme. He owns vast sisal plantations the creation of which, of course, eliminated the natural forests. But M. DeHeaulme, aware that the fauna of Madagascar was under pressure caused by the usurping or the destruction of natural habitat, decided to create, at Berenty, an oasis in the vast, serried ranks of spiky sisal plants, by fencing off an area of the virgin gallery forest along the banks of the Mandrare River. Here the forest is protected from indiscriminate grazing by zebu and from logging by man, and so the lemur colonies not only flourish, but have become so tame that they are easy to study and photograph.

As we drove through mile after mile of hot, dry sisal plantation, however, my spirits sank as I thought of how many areas of beautiful natural forest had been snuffed out to make way for a prickly, cactus-like ugly plant whose only attribute is that it provides hemp. Lee, on the other hand, grew more and more excited the nearer we got to Berenty, for this was where she had spent a lot of her time during her two years of study in Madagascar and so she knew what was in store for us.

Presently the road ran out of the sisal plantations and became lined with forest, mainly composed of huge, grey-trunked tamarind trees. These tamarinds

form the bulk of the forest at Berenty and, in fact, are not a Malagasy species, but were imported by the Arabs five or six hundred years ago. They have flourished, however, and the lemurs have adapted well to them, feeding voraciously off the leaves and fruit. The road wound through these huge, shady trees and ended at a small group of whitewashed buildings which made up the hotel and museum which M. DeHeaulme has built for visitors. Behind the buildings the thick forest began, spreading for some two hundred and forty acres along the river bank.

The author and his wife outside the gates to the special reserve of Berenty.

The magical acrobats of the tree-tops: the sifaka lemur.

The lovely and graceful sifaka lemur bounding in the trees, clinging to branches, and peering down at its strange human visitors.

As Berenty, scientifically speaking, is most famous for its beautiful ringtail troops, it was naturally these artistically designed creatures I expected to see first. But what suddenly catapulted into my life was a completely different kind of lemur, one I had never seen before, and one which, from the moment I set eyes on it, became and still is my favourite creature in Madagascar.

It fell out of a small tree at the wayside. There is no other way to describe it. But as it landed it bounced as though its hind legs were springs and bounded across the road in a series of huge, graceful hops. It was much bigger than a ringtail, and it had a black face with a picture-frame of white fur round it, a black cap, and sooty markings on its arms and legs; but the rest of its thick fur was creamy white and looked as though it had been spun out of a million dandelion clocks. It paused when it reached the other side of the road and gazed at us interestedly.

'A sifaka, a sifaka!' said Lee, excitedly. 'Look, isn't it simply beautiful?'

And indeed it was. Its sooty black face had a *retroussé* black button nose and its round eyes were golden in colour. Its face and expression reminded me in some ways of a two-toed sloth, a South American creature that I love passionately. But the sifaka really won my heart. Not only was it so attractive to look at — the quintessence of cuddliness — but its mode of progression, its great silent bouncing hops, was so enchanting and amazing. This one watched us for a moment or two and then, without any apparent muscular contraction, simply shot straight up into the air and the next second was clinging to a tree trunk some six feet from the ground, clinging so tightly it looked as though it had been grafted on. It stayed there for a moment, regarding us with its surprised golden eyes, and then left the tree propelling itself with its long hind legs, turning in mid-air so that it landed the right way round, 'grafted' on to another tree trunk some twenty feet away. Here it stayed for a few minutes and then, bored with our attentions, set off through the forest in a series of prodigious and absolutely silent leaps as easily as if it had been progressing along level ground.

Later on during our stay, I looked out of our room and saw three sifakas bounding like balls across the courtyard. Going outside, I stood under a small tree for about a quarter of an hour, watching them bounding about in the distant trees through my binoculars. Then, when I was preparing to go back into the house I glanced up and there, to my astonishment, were five sifakas lolling about in the branches above my head within touching distance. They were all in nonchalant attitudes, their long legs dangling, regarding me from grave golden eyes. Occasionally one would reach out, delicately pluck a tiny leaf and put it daintily into its mouth. It flattered me that they did not regard me as being in any way a menace — if anything I think they found me rather boring and perhaps a trifle boorish as I walked round and round the tree peering at them from every angle. But for me it was a great thrill to be so close to these enchanting animals and have them treat me as if I were not there.

Later on the day of our arrival we set off into the reserve. The only way the forest has been altered is that M. DeHeaulme has cut a series of wide paths across the whole area, rather like 'rides' in an English forest. These not only allow you to get about more quickly, but also enable you to pinpoint whereabouts you are in the area, for in that sort of tangle you can soon get lost. We found that, while there were small troops of sifakas in the forest, the bulk of the lemur population was made up of troops, some twenty strong, of ringtails. Though they wandered through the forest they also found the roadways useful, and it was most amusing to watch a troop of them ambling sedately along the road, pausing to pick up a seed or an insect, all their black-and-white-ringed tails held stiffly aloft like strange, funny caterpillars. Like the sifakas the ringtails completely ignored us, and we sat there among the trees, surrounded by feeding, bickering lemurs who appeared to regard us as just part of

A parade of Ring-tail lemurs amble down a road in Berenty.

the forest. So we could see how they marked their territory, either by using the scent gland at the base of the tail, or else by slashing grooves in the bark of branches and tree trunks with the sharp, horny wrist spurs, which also produce scent. Some older trees had their trunks slashed up to a height of three feet with hundreds of cuts, as though someone had carved a pattern with a penknife.

It was enchanting to be able to drift through the forest with the sifakas above you and the ringtails (much more terrestrial) walking all around you; and there were the other inhabitants of the forest as well.

Dozens of handsome kites gathered to bathe in the shallows on the great sand-bars that lay like fawn ribs across the glinting, chocolate-coloured waters of the river. Having bathed, they would fly to a particular very large dead tamarind tree on the edge of the forest where they would festoon the branches, holding out their wings and shuffling their feathers to let them dry in the brilliant hot sunshine. Along the paths you could see and hear the Madagascar fodies, perched in the sombre recesses of the forest, singing their delightful song, their red feathering making them stand out against the shadows like drops of blood. Then there were the great, long-tailed ground couas, and cuckoo-sized crested couas, clad in greyish blue, and an all-black coucal, devil black with bright russet wings, who made the forest ring with its liquid cries. There were five-foot-long yellow and black snakes, looking like animated old school ties; chameleons of every shape —crested, horned and otherwise bedecked; and a most peculiar insect which Lee found, the famous Malagasy 'hissing' cockroach. This large, glossy brown, prickly creature, fat and round and the size of a lemon, was beautifully armoured against its enemies. But as well, it had a trick which could make the more timid predator retreat. On being picked up it made a loud ringing-zinging noise, such as a toy clockwork train makes when lifted suddenly from its rails. The noise is so unexpected and loud that you are instinctively startled into dropping the creature.

A splash of red marks the lovely Madagascar fody perched in the forest singing its lovely song.

Our time in the enchanted forests of Berenty seemed
all too short, but we had to press on and follow Roland
to the northwest where he wanted to show us 'his'
forest, a reserve with one of those jaw-breaking Malagasy names — Ankarafantsika. This is a curious dry
deciduous tropical forest that Roland and his students
at the University of Madagascar had been studying for
some time. So we went back to Antananarivo (from
which all roads seemed to lead) and started off in our
mini-bus, packed with our gear and our persons, for
the fifteen-hour gruelling drive over extremely bad
roads. At first the countryside was the rolling uplands,
badly eroded with great red areas of exposed laterite.
Here and there in the valleys there were squares of
water denoting a rice paddy, the surface reflecting the
blue sky, the whole thing framed in a rim of emerald
green. Many times during the day we were slowed
down or brought to a halt by huge herds of zebu being
driven to market, their hooves kicking up pale-pink
swathes of dust that floated in great clouds in the still,
sunlit air. We stopped for lunch in a tiny and very
picturesque village, the small brown brick houses with
their steeply pitched roofs giving the place a curiously
Hansel-and-Gretel Tyrolean air. Here the restaurant
was in a vast upstairs room, and we fed off delicious
crab soup and *ramazava*, a sort of Malagasy Irish stew
served on rice and containing meat and chicken. It was
a delicious and sustaining meal, but unfortunately
John, who had picked up a stomach bug in Mauritius,
was unable to eat anything. As compensation I pur-
chased for him a bottle of rice brandy, manufactured in
Korea, with a whole, real viper enshrined in its
depths. Apparently this revolting drink is much
favoured by the Chinese population in Madagascar.
John was very proud of this bottle but, rather selfishly
we thought, refused to take a swig from it so we could
witness its potency. We felt sure a swig of it would put
paid to any bug he was suffering from.

Reptile in a bottle: John
Hartley holds up a revolting
brew of rice brandy.

Weary travellers take a break
in the Malagasy forest.

Finally we arrived at the village of Ampijoroa at the foot of the small escarpment on which lay the forest reserve. We found a huge and beautiful grove and here we pitched camp. At dawn the next morning the trees above our tents were full of a great chorus of birds, busily hunting through the sunlit tree-tops in search of insect life. I noticed that the bit of forest in which we had so gaily pitched our camp was in reality a most dangerous place, for the trees were of that formidable species whose trunk is completely covered with stout thorns, sharp as needles, each about two inches long. They made moving through the trees a hazard, for should you trip, you automatically put a hand out to a tree trunk to steady yourself, and immediately your hand was lacerated. What was even worse, I found, was that, unthinkingly, you would sometimes lean up against a spiky trunk to steady yourself while examining the canopy above through your binoculars. Both your shirt and your back suffered from this manoeuvre.

A flamboyant sifaka up a tree.

Peril of the forest: sharp thorns covering tree trunks are a dangerous hazard to the unwary.

This morning of our arrival I was busy dodging thorns and trying to watch birds, when a great cacophony of purring grunts broke out in the tree-tops a short distance away from me, and I could hear the swish of branches. Making my way as rapidly as I could through the forest I soon found myself standing below a group of trees in which some lemurs were feeding. Suddenly they all left the trees they were in and did an astonishing thing; they bounded through the branches *towards* me and having reached a vantage point they stopped and peered down at me. I saw that they were sifakas, but of a different and more handsome subspecies than the ones I had fallen in love with at Berenty. These seemed slightly more creamy in colour, and the insides of their forearms and thighs were a rich, glinting mahogany-chestnut. This was a beautiful combination of colours, making them very handsome and spectacular. What interested me, as I watched, was their silence. Apart from that one outburst of song, they were quite quiet. Only when they jumped onto a slender branch that bent beneath their weight did the leaves swish and give away their presence. Otherwise, silent as clouds they drifted through the forest taking enormous, bouncing jumps from tree to tree. I decided that, although the Berenty sifakas were wonderful, these, with their flamboyant coloration, were really the more beautiful.

Later that day we made our way up onto the escarpment, and, following the sandy tracks through the trees, we soon reached Roland's well-appointed camp in the heart of the forest. Here he explained to us what he and his students from the University were doing. They were, in fact, trying to piece together a portrait of the forest. A certain area had been chosen; it was then divided into areas like a chess-board by clearing a series of narrow paths. Each path had its number and this corresponded to the numbers on a map. Thus, wherever you were in the forest, by consulting the number pinned to a tree at the intersections and comparing it to the map, you knew exactly where you were. It was like saying you turn left down the Champs Elysées, right along Old Bond Street and left again at Forty-second Street. Each one of the squares thus created by this network of little paths was being studied in detail. Plants, insects, reptiles were being catalogued; birds caught in mist nets, ringed and released. There were even leaf traps, specially constructed boxes which caught falling leaves so that their density and therefore their contribution to the humus of the forest floor could be ascertained.

In addition, the lemur troops that lived in this strange dry deciduous tropical forest were being studied, and this by means of a new weapon (literally) in the armoury of the modern scientist — the dart gun. This is like a very aristocratic version of the air rifle and shoots what is, to all intents and purposes, a hypodermic syringe with a tranquilliser in it. You aim it at the animal's flank, the dart enters and within a minute or so the animal is unconscious and falls from the tree into your nets or, in some cases, your open arms. Once the animal is thus captured a small radio collar is put round its neck and then, when the specimen recovers, it is released at the place of capture. None the worse for its experience, and apparently unaware of its collar, it goes back to join its companions (if it is a gregarious species) or continues its solitary existence. But whichever it does, its every movement can be followed by the small radio in the collar which sends out a regular signal that is picked up on a portable apparatus with an aerial. The bleeps tell where the creature is and where and when it moves, and these movements can then be recorded on the map. So by walking through the forest with your radio receiver, with a minimum of difficulty you can track down all the lemur troops and study their habits.

There were two species that Roland wanted to fit collars to, and he had put off capturing them until we arrived so that we could observe and film the whole process. So that afternoon we spread out through the forest in search of a sifaka troop, and after about an hour's search we found one indulging in a siesta in a group of trees. As we congregated below them they watched us with deep interest and complete lack of fear. Roland loaded the dart gun, took careful aim at a sifaka and fired. There was a faint plop, like the noise made by an old-fashioned popgun, and the dart hit one of the lemurs accurately in the thigh. The animal jumped slightly, but more from surprise at the noise of the gun. It did not appear to even notice the dart, with its brightly coloured wool 'feathers' sticking out of its thigh. Within a minute or so its eyes seemed to get bigger, if that were possible, and it started to blink and sway. Gradually its head drooped forward, its hands and feet relaxed their hold on the branches, and it slid down and we caught it gently before it hit the ground. They were lovely creatures to see at a distance, but to have the opportunity to examine one at close quarters was a rare privilege. The fur was dense, soft and woolly and the chestnut red on the arms and legs was even more pronounced close to. The hands and feet were beautifully adapted for grasping, and the skin was black and so soft that any woman would have been envious of its velvety texture. The great eyes were the beautiful shade of a bronze chrysanthemum and were wide open, staring out unseeingly, for the animal was completely unconscious. Rapidly Roland fixed the little leather collar with the transmitter round its neck. We then placed the creature in a bag and left it in a cool, shady place to recover. Within a couple of hours it had revived sufficiently to be released, and it scrambled up the trees a little shakily to rejoin its companions, unaware that its transmitter was flooding Roland's receiver with a steady series of high-pitched 'bleeps'.

An Avahi. A nocturnal lemur, its eyes glowing in the torch beams at night.

Our second hunt took place after dark with headlights, for our quarry was one of the smaller, nocturnal lemurs called an avahi. (There are actually seven different species of lemur in this large and important forest, but our short time there only allowed us to see two.) We were lucky, for we had only gone a short distance into the forest before we found a couple of avahis, sitting together in a tangle of creepers, their eyes glowing in our light beams. However, if finding them had been easy, darting them was a different matter, for the floodlight cast numerous flickering shadows, and the avahis themselves were anything but co-operative. They were not afraid of us, but were very lively and kept leaping from tree to tree. Never-theless after several abortive shots Roland finally darted one, and very soon it was in our hands. It was a charming creature, about the size of a large domestic cat, with dense grey-green fur, a pale-grey belly, a russet-coloured tail and a grey mask on its face from which its eyes stared like two golden guineas. It had a very rounded head, accentuated by the fact that its neat little ears were buried in the deep fur of its head. Again I was amazed at the beautifully adapted hands and feet and, above all, at their silky softness. You would think that creatures who spend their time leap-ing and running through trees with rough bark would have hands which were calloused and rough instead of being infinitely softer than any baby's bottom. Soon the avahi, with his collar on, was back in the forest and we left him to his nightly activities.

It was a pity that our time was limited in Ankarafantsika, but we had to press on for there were many other fascinating and bizarre areas of Madagas-car we wanted to visit and many other strange creatures to meet.

Nosy Komba
and the
Crocodile Dance

Without doubt one of the driest, most inimical and most fantastic habitats I have ever seen delicate-looking animals living in was the great thorny forest area of southern Madagascar. Firstly, of course, it is not forest in the accepted sense of the word, for it is made up of several gigantic plants found only in Madagascar and all resembling in some ways the cacti of other parts of the world. The chief species of the forest (*Alluaudia procera*) has a thick trunk from which fountains upward a series of long, whippy, green fingers that grow to a height of some seventy-five feet. Each of these astonishing rubbery limbs is covered with small, circular, fleshy green leaves the size of your thumb-nail. These grow in rows round and round the limbs, and between each leaf is set a long, needle-sharp pine, an inch long and as tough as steel. The ground underneath this lethal canopy has a number of other low-growing species, each armed with its own carefully evolved battery of spikes. There is one delightful species that looks like a round length of green plastic tubing, jointed together and bestrewn with spokes. The plant looks tough but breaks easily, exuding a white, milky substance which can blind you if it gets in your eyes. This weird green landscape was the sort of forest that a science fiction writer would locate on some remote planet like Mars or Venus. You would not think that such creatures as lemurs could have adapted to live in such a malevolent green-barbed-wire entanglement, but they have.

We drove out to a little cattle township called Hazofotsy over a bone-splintering road. After travelling through the Malagasy countryside we had been used to, we were suddenly, without warning, plunged into the thorny forest. The rutted road ran through the serried ranks of alluaudias, which lifted their admonishing prickly fingers to the sky, their thorns glittering like amber needles in the sun, their rows of tiny, fleshy leaves looking jade-green against the hot blue sky. We

had driven, I suppose, some six or seven miles into
this weird forest when, slowing down to avoid a particularly large pot-hole, we heard a gruff, chanting cry
that sounded familiar. We stopped and got out onto
the dusty road. Listening we heard the cry again, in
the undergrowth alongside the road. It sounded just
like the cry of the sifaka, but surely, I thought to
myself, such a dainty acrobatic and arboreal mammal
could not exist here. But I was wrong. Quietly I picked
my way into the dim, thorny interior and then passed
beneath a huge alluaudia that looked the sort of plant
the Spanish Inquisition would have designed, and
waited for the animals to call again. After waiting,
talking in whispers for some ten minutes, I happened
to glance directly above us and found to my embar-
rassment that squatting in the branches six feet over
our heads was a troop of six snow-white sifakas,
regarding us with interest from large golden eyes.
Incredibly, they clung to the spiky branches without
any apparent discomfort, and when they saw that we
had spotted them, they made off in a series of prodigious bounds, landing hard enough on the alluaudia
branches to bend them over and paying no more
attention to the spikes than if they had been constructed of rubber. I have seen a great many animals in
many parts of the world cope with a hazardous habitat, but never anything to compare with this.

We drove on, and towards evening we came to the
dusty, tumble-down cluster of huts and corrals that
was Hazofotsy. We camped a little way away from the
village on the banks of a small dried-up stream bed.
The following morning when we awoke, the chief of
the settlement came to visit us, bringing a bottle of
fresh warm zebu milk for our breakfast. Then we set
off to explore the forest, and before long we came
across another of its inhabitants. It was Lee who spotted the nest of leaves wedged in a thorny vine-covered
cleft between alluaudia branches. She found a long

The strange landscape of
alluaudia trees in the great
thorny forest area of southern
Madagascar.

The unusual pot-bellied
baobab tree, of which there
are nine species in
Madagascar.

thornless twig and gently touched the nest with it, and the next moment there appeared two diminutive and adorable-looking creatures, smaller than newly born kittens. Their fur was pale ash grey, so that their long, furry tails looked like delicate plumes of smoke. They had almost transparent ears of pinky-grey, enormous liquid brown eyes, and dainty little hands and feet. They were mouse lemurs, the smallest of the Primates — three of them would have fitted comfortably into an average teacup and still have left enough room for a couple of lumps of sugar. They scrambled up on top of their house and stared down at us with huge eyes, looking like very lilliputian owls. Then, deciding we might be potentially dangerous, they fled through the forest like miniature ballet dancers, leaping and pirouetting with uncanny skill, like someone dancing through a room full of rapiers. Later we found several more of these leaf nests, but none of them were inhabited.

At one point in the forest we found and photographed a strange species of tortoise, the spider tortoise. This strange beast has the scales of the rim of its shell protruding in spikes, so it fitted in very well with thorny forest background. In places there were clearings among the armoured ranks of the alluaudia, and here grew baobab trees. This is one of the most unusual and endearing trees in Madagascar, with an immense pot-bellied silver trunk and a silly little cluster of minute twisted branches covered with green leaves that looked like a very badly designed and inadequate wig on a very large woman. Madagascar has nine species of this rotund and ridiculous-looking tree, whereas Africa has only one. In parts of the forest we found baobab corpses, trees that had been felled and their pot-bellies split open so that cattle could mumble and chew the trunk to extract the water that was stored in it. Seeing the carcasses of these giant trees was very depressing, for they had taken centuries to grow and were felled in a day to provide maybe a few bucketsful of water for the ever-present and destructive zebu. Moreover this was one of Madagascar's largest reserves, where tree felling was forbidden, as was the grazing of cattle. But when we discovered that this vast reserve was policed (if one can use that term) by one man who lived 30 miles away and had no transport to patrol the reserve with, we were not surprised that the local people treated the area with scant respect. Looking at the living baobabs, their tummies the circumference of a small room, their idiotic little branches twisted against the sky, I was reminded of the African folk-tale that relates how once the baobab was as other trees, but then it offended God, and so He, in His wrath, plucked it from the soil and replanted it upside down. That is why the baobab has such spindly branches, for they are really roots.

As night fell the forest was full of the noise of insects and the pulsating greenish light of fireflies. It was then we heard the weird, eldritch screech of yet another species of lemur, the strictly nocturnal lepilemur. Roland wanted to trap one of these creatures so that he could put a radio collar on it and study its movements, but in the thorny forest it was difficult to move around and get a clear shot with the dart gun, so we were forced to use other methods. We were joined by two stalwart young hunters from Hazofotsy armed with long poles to the end of which were attached nooses of string. By this means the Malagasy have been trapping lepilemurs since time immemorial. We set off with our torches and made our way through the forest, our light beams illuminating the strange alluaudia fronds, so that it seemed as if we were making our way through some deep dark pond with a monstrous weed growth. We could hear the lepilemurs screeching all around us, and it was not long before our hunters had spotted one, its eyes gleaming red in our torch beams. While we dazzled it with our lights they edged their poles nearer and nearer to the hypnotised creature and then slipped a noose over its head. A firm tug, and there was the animal, the noose around its neck, clinging to the pole and protesting at this treatment with a series of harsh, ear-splitting screams that made one's blood run cold. Quickly they lowered it to the ground where Roland deftly put the radio collar on. Within a couple of minutes we had released the creature and it bounded away through the alluaudias as sure-footedly as if it had been broad daylight, uttering moaning shrieks at the indignity we had made it suffer.

A close examination of the hand of a lepilemur shows the opposed thumb and forefingers, giving a maximum of gripping power to this versatile creature.

I had examined the lepilemur in the torch light, of course, but this is never the best light for seeing the colours of an animal, and so I was delighted when, the following day, Roland came across a lepilemur in an accessible place and managed to dart it to put a collar on. This gave me the chance of examining it with care. It was about half the size of a large cat and its soft grey fur was so dense that it looked as though it had been clipped. The pale ears were set close in the fur of the head and the eyes were enormous and marigold-yellow in colour, slightly protuberant. The thumbs on both its hands and feet were widely opposed to the forefingers, thus giving maximum gripping power, and the delicate tips of each finger were pressed out into small circular discs that looked like suckers. These soft pads, of course, were the braking mechanism. When the animal hurled itself from one tree to another, these pads acted as a brake as it landed. A curious but not obvious thing about the lepilemur is its enormous caecum, that part of the stomach—small in human beings—from which the appendix grows. Owing to its fibrous diet of alluaudia leaves the lepilemur's caecum is enormous compared to the size of a human's. In fact if a human had a caecum proportionately as big, you could truthfully say he or she had the equivalent of three stomachs in one.

After a fascinating few days spent in this unbelievably harsh but beautiful terrain, we moved northward to pay a visit to an area that could not have been more different, the lush tropical island of Nosy Komba which lay in the brilliant blue sea off the northwest coast of Madagascar. We were particularly anxious to visit Nosy Komba not simply because it was an island, but because it was the home of a special species of lemur which was sacred to the islanders, as many species of lemur in Madagascar had been at one time, and thus earning themselves immunity from persecution. Now, unfortunately, most of the beliefs in the lemurs' magical powers have died out, except in remote places such as this island.

A view showing the beauty of Nosy Komba

It was a beautiful day when we set out in our launch, and the sun burnished the sea in swathes of palest cornflower-blue from which, at intervals, flying fish burst like rockets to shoot through the air, ruling a straight line with their drooping tails along the surface of the sea. After some two hours we could see the humpback of Nosy Komba appearing, furry with rain forest picked out in a dozen shades of green and russet. We rounded a headland and made towards a long golden beach lined with palm trees, among which we could make out the huts of the village. The launch's engine stammered to a halt, and in the silence we drifted shoreward until pulled up short by the anchor. We unloaded the food we had brought into the dinghy, for you never arrive at small remote islands and become a liability to their limited commissariat. As we neared the beach the drums started, and as the bows of the dinghy scrunched softly into the sand and we stepped out into the lukewarm sea, the entire village, clad in multicoloured robes, playing drums and twanging *valihas*, poured out of the trees and down to the beach to greet us. It was like being engulfed by a moving flower-bed, so colourful and brilliant were the costumes. The oldest lady in the village, who must have been getting on to eighty, singled me out, presuming by my grey hairs and corpulence that I must be the leader of the party, and we were soon dancing our impromptu hula up the beach together. Lee and John were similarly treated by a young village blood and a buxom maiden and so within a very short time, we literally danced our way into the village, surrounded by the grinning, clapping, dancing people. It was one of the warmest and friendliest greetings I have had anywhere in the world, and my dancing could not have been greeted with more reverence and delight if I had been Fred Astaire.

While the villagers set about the preparation of the

The island children gave the expedition a noisy welcome on the beach at Nosy Komba.

food we had brought, we made our way to the edge of the village, armed with a gift of bananas, to visit the sacred lemurs. These are the black lemurs, or Macaco lemurs, and their history is curious. Legend has it that hundreds of years ago a Malagasy king came to Nosy Komba and made it his kingdom. Among the many goods and chattels he brought with him were several black lemurs as pets for his children. Naturally, as the royal offspring's animals, they were accorded sacred status, and could in no way be molested. Under this benign regime the lemurs flourished, and their wants were attended to by a special lemur keeper who made

sure that the animals lacked for nothing. Gradually, the royal family died out but the cult of the sacred lemurs remained, as did the post of lemur keeper, which is still handed down from father to son or daughter. In this instance, the keeper of the lemurs was a handsome, shy girl of about twenty, holding a fat brown interested baby in her arms. We gave her the small, prescribed amount which you paid towards their upkeep, and she led us into the forest at the edge of the village. In the shade of the great trees she paused and called, but this was really unnecessary, for the bright-eyed lemurs had already seen us, and the trees were full of them, parading along the branches towards us, uttering loud purring grunts, tails aloft. At first glance one would be pardoned for thinking that they represented two species, so different were the sexes in appearance. The males were satanic black from head to tail, and against this dark fur their yellow eyes showed up like dandelions on a pool of pitch. The females were mainly biscuit-brown, with paler silvery-beige overtones here and there. In both sexes the fur round their faces grew in a long, tattered Elizabethan ruff, which gave them an unkempt and slightly raffish look.

They welcomed us to their kingdom with great benevolence and lack of condescension. They simply poured out of the trees and surrounded us, uttering their loud purring grunts, standing on their hind legs to pull at our trouser legs or hands, beseeching us for bananas. As this bounty was distributed, they grew more excited and even bolder, climbing up our arms to sit on our shoulders or on our heads and bickering among each other over the fruit. One large male, black as a thunder-cloud, decided that the best vantage point was on top of the cine camera, so he shinned up the tripod and sat on top of the apparatus, his thick bell-rope tail hanging down over the lens, making photography impossible.

There was an extraordinary peacefulness and happiness about the atmosphere on the island.

The curious lemurs
of Nosy Komba.

After a while, when the largesse of bananas ran out, the royal lemurs grew bored with us and retreated to the great shady trees at the edge of the forest, where they paraded up and down swinging their tails, or else lay spread-eagled on the branches, their arms and legs dangling. Some went to sleep while others assiduously groomed them. Seeing them lying there in the dappled shade, relaxed and unafraid, and knowing they could enter and parade through the village without harm was a wonderful thing. Here on this idyllic island, man and animal had come to live together without rancour and animosity. One wished that lemurs all over Madagascar were accorded this right.

By the time we had finished our audience with the lemurs, the villagers had prepared the feast. As we had been admiring the lemurs, in the background we had been aware of a faint noise, steady as a heartbeat. This had been three young girls gathered round a huge wooden mortar, wielding wooden pestles to husk the rice we had brought. Rhythmic as a dance, their heavy pestles rose and fell, and as each pestle was of a different size and weight so each gave out a different sound as it struck, as church bells do. So our food was prepared to the rhythmic, three note chimes of the pestle and mortar. And what a delicious meal it was with fish, chicken and zebu served on great mountains of rice which, fortunately, had never seen the inside of a packet or a supermarket. Grey as smoke and with a lovely nutty flavour it clung, glutinous and delicious, to your teeth. Then there were bananas yellow as saffron, mangoes golden and juicy, and slabs of fresh coconut as white as snow. To wash down this gargantuan repast were beer, various soft drinks and palm wine. The last of these looked and tasted not unlike slightly acid barley water and was deceptively mild but had a kick like a mule. After such a meal what else could one do but sing and dance? So the band started up and the rhythmic clapping formed the percussion.

Numerous elegant dances were performed and then my eighty-year-old girl-friend took the floor, and in spite of the food and the palm wine (or maybe because of it) I took the floor as well. I am not sure what the dance was called, but it was a dance of seduction and left little if anything to the imagination. At the climax my sarong (which I had donned for the feast) fell gracefully to my ankles, thus putting the finishing touches to a dance that would, I am sure, have had Freud fascinated and added much to his knowledge of human behaviour.

My unexpected dance partner, one of the oldest inhabitants in the main village on the island.

The next dance was a much more vigorous and difficult one, called the crocodile dance. It was also a rather sad dance when you realised that the last crocodiles in this area had been exterminated some hundred and fifty years ago, so the dance represented (and very graphically) the movements of a creature that none of the villagers could have seen.

First a sarong or cloth was laid in the centre of the circle of villagers, the ballroom as it were. Then the two people who were to do the dance (both men) lay down flat on their stomachs opposite each other. They raised their bodies off the ground on the palms of their hands and their toes. In this awkward 'press-up' position they proceeded to jerk themselves across the grass in a series of little jumps. Finally one of them reached the cloth and, seizing it in his teeth, proceeded in this jerky way backwards, dragging the cloth. The other 'crocodile' went in hot pursuit and seized the other end of the cloth. Then a tug of war ensued until one crocodile, exhausted, fell flat on his face. John, whose lack of knowledge of the art of dancing is second only to my own, decided that, as a herpetologist, the crocodile dance was for him; and so, to the delight of the assembled company, he lowered his lanky length to the ground and challenged the winning 'crocodile'. The result had everyone in paroxysms of mirth, for John started in great style and even seized the cloth, but then his hands and toes kept giving out and, as an additional hazard, his glasses kept misting over or actually falling off so he could not see where his protagonist was. But after half an hour of this, when John gave up exhausted, the villagers gave us to understand that he was, as far as they were concerned, the best crocodile of all.

John Hartley starting to per-
form the crocodile dance.

The sun was going down in a great cluster of delicate feathery pink clouds, and the sea was as smooth as blue cream. Reluctantly we had to leave Nosy Komba, with its charming people and its entrancing lordly lemurs. The whole village, playing instruments, clapping and singing, accompanied us down to the beach and pushed the dinghy off. We reached the launch, the engine roared into life and we slid over the smooth waters. Behind us the multicoloured crowd of villagers stood on the sea's edge waving, and above the noise of the engine we could hear their singing and clapping. It was a magical experience to be so privileged as to meet people and animals in such a setting.

Lament
of the
Rain Forest

Our time in Madagascar was drawing to a close and we were most anxious to see and film two more things, a piece of the island's wonderful tropical forest and the indri, largest and most spectacular of all the lemurs. Luckily for us the tropical forest we wanted to see was the indri's home, and so we set out from Antananarivo to drive across to Perinet, the little forest reserve in which the indri lived.

At first we drove through the rolling uplands with paddy fields glittering in the sun, but then as we descended, these rolling eroded hills gave place to thicker and thicker forest. Here the great trees reared up, their branches made into miniature gardens by the epiphytes and orchids that grew along them in snakes' nests of entwined lianas. Here and there the forest was broken by a stream which glittered and frothed round moss-wigged rocks, and here and there on the banks the tree-ferns clustered like bizarre and beautiful golden-green frozen fountains. It was here that you realised how fantastic and rich this country was. In Madagascar, every tree or bush you saw was probably unique to the island and formed a wonderful, intricate habitat for the strange fauna. Here you could find the world's largest and smallest chameleons side by side. Here were carnivorous plants that trapped insects, and cacti that climbed. Here was the famous orchid with so deep and complex a throat that a moth which has evolved a six-inch proboscis is the only insect that can pollinate it. To facilitate this process the delicate creamy star-like flowers gleam luminescently in the gloom of the forest to guide the insect to its fragrant hearts. Here you can find beetles and horned spiders of such bizarre shapes and colours that the works of Fabergé fade into insignificance. Here are butterflies and moths with wings bigger than your hand, marked and intricately coloured like fine tapestries, Persian carpets or the stained glass of a hundred cathedrals. Here are insects that look so like sticks you could be pardoned for starting a fire with them; and the larvae of other insects, trailing gossamer white filaments, which look so like flowers you could attempt to fill a vase with them. Here you have frogs in liveries that would make the servants at any royal court look drab, and the lethargic chameleon who changes colour slowly and delicately as if every tiny scale were an opal. Then the mammals, strange little carnivores like a cross between a weasel and a squirrel who call to each other in tuneful and beautiful whistles; lemurs of every shape and colour; hedgehog-like tenrecs decked out in bizarre spines and hair. Then in the trees with the lemurs a panoply of birds—pigeons with bare, scarlet faces and beetle-iridescent blue-green bodies; giant couas, cornflower- and ultramarine-blue like bits of errant sky in the forest gloom; birds with monstrous beaks and birds with ravishing song and birds of sunset colouring. All this treasure in the great rain forests of Madagascar, but rain forests that—if they continue to be destroyed—will vanish in forty years or less, taking all the treasure with them, altering climate, no longer able to combat erosion, leaving the land and the people destitute. To preserve his country, the most important single thing the Malagasy must do is to preserve the forests.

After travelling for several hours we stopped in one of the charming Malagasy villages for breakfast. Delicious smells wafted to us from the open-air stalls that lined the street, and in the cool morning air, with the newly arisen sun crisping every colour, we feasted royally on fried banana cakes and fried doughnuts and drank the milk of green coconuts which was as cold as if it had been in a fridge. Three hours later we bumped down a road thickly lined with bushes weighed down with their moon-white trumpet-shaped flowers, and came into the main square of Perinet, a cluster of very dilapidated buildings. Dominating this, grandiose in design and structure, was the station hotel, for Perinet

These curious and exotic
chameleons are some of the
45 species found nowhere
else but in Madagascar.

was an important stop on the railway to the coast. The reason we had decided not to travel to Perinet by train — it was very tempting for train connoisseurs — was that the trains' times suffered from all the vagaries of the English weather, and enchanting though such a lackadaisical and relaxed approach can be, we had not the time to spare. However, to stay at the railway hotel was the next best thing. We were captivated by the hotel the moment we saw it. Seedy was not the right word for it. It had a sort of decaying grandeur about it that was irresistible. 'Here am I,' it seemed to say, 'an aristocrat, a Malagasy Gare du Nord, left here, abandoned with the forest invading me, my fabric falling apart, beset and bewildered by trains that arrive at the wrong times. Nevertheless, I welcome you to such as I have to offer.' And this marvellous station hotel had a lot to offer. There was the gigantic dining-room lined with windows, some of which looked out on to the sad square, and others out on to the main platform and the weed-grown track. It had a host of tables, a fumed oak bar with an imposing array of bottles, all empty, and massive fumed-oak beams overhead supporting art nouveau chandeliers beset with chains and cracked

Malagasy Gare du Nord

glass. The wall had once had brightly coloured murals depicting Malagasy life, but these were now dim, spider be-webbed and peeling. A broad and elegant staircase led to the upper floors where wide wooden corridors, bent and rheumatic with age, creaked and moaned protestingly at your weight. So what if the bedrooms had been painted as dark as a cave by dusty and dirty handmarks, the bed was as soft as any dried river bed, and the bath, which trickled brown water filled with mosquito larvae, looked as though it had been used as a dip for uncomplaining sheep? Outside in the mango trees mouse lemurs squeaked and trilled, giant moths like Chinese kites flew through your window and huge beetles like iridescent green leaves lurked beneath your bed. What ardent naturalist could complain, particularly when we had a handsome, beautifully mannered Malagasy manager who had the indefinable air of having been a head-waiter at the Ritz, who would get up at four in the morning to chop wood and light the kitchen fire so we could breakfast at five? Where in all the world could you find a hotel manager who would do that?

Having had a zoological if not a very restful night, we descended, yawning, at five o'clock to the dining-room and endeavoured to make ourselves feel human by the application of hot coffee and toast. Then we drove a few miles into the forest in the apple-green dawn light, amongst trees lashed together by spiders' webs bigger than cart-wheels, each sequinned with dew. We arrived at the little cluster of foresters' huts and discussed with the men the possibility of seeing and filming indri. They were quite hopeful for they said a small troop of the big lemur had been seen three days running about two miles from the huts. While we set off into the forest to try our luck we asked the foresters and their children (for children are excellent at locating creatures) if they would collect some of the lesser denizens of the forest for us to film.

The handsome and harmless
Madagascan Boa we filmed.

The path that led into the forest climbed a steep
slope in which the foresters had cut steps and propped
them with cut logs. At the top it flattened out and
meandered off through the thick forest. Here again
were the giant dew-spangled spiders' webs, each with
its fantastic occupant; these crab-shaped spiders, with
bodies the size of a damson, were clad in crimson,
gold, white and yellow, and on the ends of their abdo-
mens had great, curved decorations like miniature
zebu horns. The tops of the trees were still entwined
with skeins of mist drawn out by the rising sun, and
the leaves around us were full of the chorus of unseen
birds.

We knew that the indris are the aristocrats of the
lemurs, and, as befits those of noble lineage, they
rarely get up much before ten o'clock when the mist
has lifted and the forest is, so to speak, aired and
warm. Then they move slowly round their territory in
a series of prodigious kangaroo-like leaps from tree to
tree, feeding on the fresh green leaves, flowers and
shoots and pausing periodically to delineate their
kingdom with the aid of their powerful and beautiful
song. So we walked slowly and quietly through the
forest, hoping to find the indris' boudoir before they
had arisen, and so be in a position to track their
movements for the rest of the morning. But half past
nine came and we still had had no success. We knew
that unless we pinpointed the indris by ten o'clock
they would be on the move, and we could wander
haphazardly all over the forest all day without finding
them.

But try as we would we could not locate our quarry,
and at eleven o'clock we had to give up and make our
way back to the foresters' huts. Here we were slightly
mollified by the smaller prizes that had been obtained
for us. There were two species of chameleon, one a
dragon-green monster as long as my forearm from
wrist to elbow, with a fat tail coiled like a green Cather-

ine wheel, parrot-like feet and wildly swivelling eyes. The other was smaller, banded in coffee-brown and pale putty, with a raised casque on his head resembling the armoured headgear of an ancient knight, and a serrated edge along his backbone. The foresters' children had also captured a handsome olive-green and black Madagascar boa some six feet long. He proved to be a most tractable and charming snake and let us photograph him from every conceivable angle, climbing and wriggling about various parts of the forest. After an hour, however, he felt he had done sufficient acting and started to hiss at us in a peevish sort of way. We felt he had been most patient and deserved his freedom, and so we let him go and filmed him as he disappeared into the forest.

Another creature the children had obtained was one I had long wanted to meet, the Malagasy pill-millipede or, as it is called in England, the wood-louse. But in Europe these harmless and enchanting creatures only grow to the size of a plump garden pea, whereas in Madagascar they grow to the size of a billiard ball. I don't quite know where the fascination for pygmy or giant things lies, but I know I was delighted with the handful of pill-millipedes the children had caught. These were rolled into a ball, and their 'shells' were a lovely shade of greenish black, each joint picked out with a pale yellow stripe at the 'hinge'. The size of small plums, they had the smooth feel of something machine-turned. Placed on the ground they would remain unmoving for a moment or two and then slowly uncurl, displaying their forest of ginger legs on the underside. With an effort they would set their rotund bodies the right way up and then, all their legs working overtime, they would trundle off, looking more like clockwork toys than real creatures.

For three days we wandered the forests of Perinet without contacting indris, and we were beginning to lose hope of filming them. Once, on the very edge of

Lying on its back with its legs in the air the Madagascan giant Millipede, the size of a ping-pong ball.

John Hartley sits quietly in the forest at Perinet.

sound, like the shadow of an echo, we heard a troop
singing many miles from us, but that was all. We had
quartered our section of the forest pretty thoroughly
but with no success and we now had to make up our
minds whether to move to a different area and start
again. We decided to give our section of forest one
more try. So we went through the ritual —breakfast at
dawn, climbing the escarpment half asleep, and then,
in the early sun's rays, quartering the forest. At ten
o'clock, dispirited, we assembled at a gigantic tree that
was a landmark on the path. Its dark- and pale-green
leaves framed huge branches of magenta-pink
flowers, glowing against the blue sky. Depressed, we
drank and ate some food and discussed the situation.
Because of our timetable it was impossible now, we
felt, to move to another area, and yet this area had
proved to be no use. It seemed as if we were doomed
not to film indri.

But then, just as we were starting to pack up to go
back to the hotel, we were all startled, to say the least,
by a sudden ear-splitting, ground-vibrating, roaring,
howling chorus that broke out directly over our heads.
The noise was indescribable and made the forest
vibrate like a harp. Moving our vantage point we could
see, thirty feet above us, taking their ease in the sunlit
garden of pink flowers, a troop of five indri, open-
mouthed, singing their territorial chorus. It had all the
rich, sonorous quality of organ music, but —as I later
discovered— it sounded much more like the weird
and beautiful calls of whales.

We could not believe our luck. There, in full sunlight
sat the indris, each as large as a three-year-old child,
decked out handsomely in their black and white fur
with wildly staring chrysanthemum-yellow eyes and
shaggy ear plumes. In between reverberating
choruses they paused to pluck leaves and stuff them
into their pink mouths.

Presently, finding the supply of food dwindling,

they hurled themselves into the forest. There is no other description. Clinging to a vertical branch, an indri would simply bunch its powerful hind legs under it and launch itself like a furry black and white projectile. As it flew backwards, it would turn in mid-air so that when it landed on another tree it was facing the right way, and now the hind legs could cushion the landing. Apart from the length of these prodigious leaps what amazed us most was the silence of them, for these huge lemurs propelled themselves at speed through the forest with scarcely a rustle to betray their presence. That they had no fear of us was obvious — they were too concerned with obtaining their breakfast and singing. One female, in fact, spotting some succu-lent leaves, came down a sapling, looking ridiculously like a wooden toy monkey on a stick, and started feeding within two feet of the ground and within six feet of me and Lee.

So we followed the troop for most of the morning until, tiring of our attentions, they bounded off into the forest and disappeared. Although for sheer charm the sifaka still held my heart, I was deeply impressed by the dignity and beauty and self-confidence of the indri. It was a privilege to share the world with such an animal, but for how long could we do so? If the forests vanish — and they *are* vanishing — the indri goes with them.

The morning before we left, Lee and I walked up the road towards the forest and stood listening to the indris, as the sky turned from green to blue. Their haunting, wonderful, mournful song came to us, plaintive, beautiful and sad. It could have been the very voice of the forest, the very voice of Madagascar lamenting.

The biggest and most spectacular of the lemurs, the handsome Indri, singers of the forest.

Index

Acknowledgements

ARK ON THE MOVE,
a thirteen-part television series
A Nielsen-Ferns International Ltd. Production
in association with the Canadian Broadcasting Corporation,
Primetime Television   Channel Television
South African Broadcasting Corporation and the
Australian Broadcasting Commission

International Distribution by
Richard Price Television Associates,
Seymour Mews House
Seymour Mews
Wigmore Street
London W1H 9PE
U.K.

PHOTOGRAPHS

Quentin Bloxam
J.B. Caroll
Phillip Coffey
Lee Durrell
John Hartley
Michael Maltby
William Oliver

MAPS

Acorn Technical Art Inc., Toronto

All over the world hundreds of species of animals are facing extinction due to the direct or indirect interference of man.

The destruction of wild animal life increasingly threatens the vital natural balance between man and his environment and has dire implications to future life, both human and animal, on this planet.

We at the Wildlife Preservation Trust are trying to do something about this dismal situation before it is too late

The Trust is devoted entirely to the concept of captive breeding of endangered species as one means of ensuring their survival. Rescue operations are being mounted on an ongoing basis to save animal species. We study their biology in order to learn how to preserve them in captivity and conserve them in the wild.

Once sufficient numbers have been bred in captivity, groups can be sent back to increase the world population. In some cases, where species are down to a handful of specimens in the world, this vital work may save them from extinction.

Our task is to make certain that as few species as possible disappear from our world. The task is immense, but we at the Trust believe we can succeed, if we gain the support and interest of more and more people. If you are interested in helping to save the animals and would like more information about our work at the Trust and live in the U.S.A. please write to me at:

    Wildlife Preservation Trust International
    34th Street and Girard Avenue
    Philadelphia, Pa. 19104

or if you live elsewhere in the world write to me at:

    Jersey Wildlife Preservation Trust
    Les Augrés Manor
    Trinity
    Jersey
    Channel Islands